How to Deliver "Suck-free" Online Meetings

An Easy Step-by-Step Guide to Planning and Running Effective Online Meetings

Edition 1.2

Benjamin Pitman, Ph.D.

Library of Congress Cataloging-in-Publication Data
Pitman Ph.D., Benjamin.
How to Deliver "Suck-free" Online Meetings
ISBN: 9798579164353   .

Thanks

To the Order of St. Luke for allowing me to help them out and write the beginning papers on how to use Zoom for their teams.

To Covid 19. As one person said, it would be a shame to go through all this pain and not have any gain. If it weren't for the virus, we would still be at the beginnings of online meetings.

And of course, my wife, Sharon, who contributed many of the ideas in this book and her ongoing loving support.

And to Theo S., an Amazon Kindle Support Rep, who caught a typo on the way to publication.

A Special Thanks

To Eric Anderson, a long-time friend who granted me several interviews and gave me insights, perspectives, and ideas that otherwise would have been left in the great unknown.

About the Author

Ben Pitman built self-paced online training called e-learning—training courses that people would take by themselves at a computer on the job. He has authored several books on the subject (below). He holds a Ph.D. in Human Resource Development.

Effective eLearning Design series:

Vol. 1: Designing Effective eLearning: A Step-by-Step Guide

Vol. 2: Superb eLearning using Low-Cost Scenarios: A Step-by-Step Guide to eLearning by Doing

Vol. 3: Converting Classroom Training to eLearning: A Step-by-Step Guide for when You Get Stuck with It

Mastering Lectora® series:

Vol. 1: Lectora 101: Ten Easy Steps for Beginners

Vol. 2: Lectora 201: What They Don't Tell You in Class

Vol. 3: Lectora 301: Techniques for Professionals

Contents

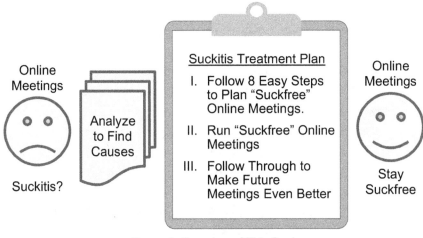

Figure 1: Overview of This Book

Why This Book?

The number of online meetings is skyrocketing due to the pandemic, traffic, convenience, and technology. **Most of these meetings have a significant "suck factor."** They have varying degrees of "Suckitis."

People are leaving online meetings feeling dissatisfied and dreading the next one. Meeting goals and objectives may be met, but relationships that used to be created and strengthened in meetings are suffering. People have a vague feeling that something was missing, something just below the surface, something that they can't quite put their finger on. As this continues, anxiety increases—and most people are barely aware of this part.

Online meetings are certainly better than no meetings at all. But when relationships suffer, so does trust. As trust declines, so does productivity and sales. *"The world runs on trust."* Don't take my word for it. Just look around.

> **I believe with the right information, you can *easily* have much better, more effective online meetings. The purpose of this book is to help you see why many online meetings suck and then help you plan and run highly effective, highly rewarding online meetings.**

To do this, it takes more than the "Seven Magic Steps to an Effective Meeting" in someone's blog.

✓ It takes a deeper **understanding** of the **causes** of "Suckitis."

✓ It takes **know-how** to **plan** online meetings that take into account the causes of "Suckitis."

✓ It takes **different know-how** and focused attention to **run** online meetings that do not suck.

This book will give you that understanding and know-how.

All you need is to be aware of things you would otherwise take for granted, stick to your agenda, and do whatever you can to keep people engaged and build relationships.

What This Book Is NOT About

It is not about managing conflict in meetings, team building, how to use any meeting app like Zoom, Google Meet, etc., or how to broadcast on Facebook.

It is less about the kind of meetings you broadcast on Facebook or other online channels where there is little if any participation. *However, a great deal of this book does apply to those meetings.*

PART 1: DIAGNOSIS

This book uses the medical paradigm to approach making online meetings suck less than they do today.

PART 1: DIAGNOSIS **performs an analysis** on the patient (online meetings) to determine what is wrong and formulate a diagnosis. We use a model to give us a framework to base our analysis on rather than just shooting in the wind and grabbing on to various aspects of a meeting that we might need to fix. This analysis reveals 45 differences between in-person meetings and online ones.

PART 2: TREATMENT PLAN **develops a three-stage treatment plan** based on the diagnosis to cure as much as possible the "Suckitis," addressing the design of a meeting, running it, and following through after the meeting. In this part, you will see:

> Driving Principles: Look like this. They form the basis of the treatment plan. They explain how things work. These are cause and effect relationships.

> Guideline: **Guidelines are driving principles in action. They direct you in designing the meeting plan (agenda), like what to include, length, and what to focus on.**

 Best Practice: **Best practices are something you could practice, like running a breakout room session or recording a meeting. A "Best Practice" would not affect your agenda.**

Common Problem 1: Common problems look like this. They are listed along with some ideas about how to fix them.

 Warning: Warnings look like this. These are just a heads up, so you don't make the same mistake others have.

But before we get started, I'd like you to make some very brief notes that we will come back to at the end of the book. You probably have been in or have led online meetings that seemed to be less than optimal; otherwise, you wouldn't be reading this book. So, *briefly* write down:

What do you think is wrong with the online meetings you've attended or led? What made them not-so-good?

What would you personally like to know how to do better in these meetings?

Since you are probably a busy person with many other things on your mind, put these somewhere where you can find them a month from now when you finally finish the book ☺. Maybe on a sheet of paper in the last chapter of the book or if, you're using Kindle, put them as a note at the beginning of the last chapter.

We will begin by listening to our patient (online meetings) to see if there is a problem.

Chapter 1

Do Our Online Meetings Have "Suckitis"?

Is There an Online Meeting Pandemic Too?

Some Indications

Covid 19 drove me to attend many online meetings. After the novelty wore off, I realized that they were beginning to suck. The meetings sort of worked but not quite. Was I alone thinking this? A quick search of the internet revealed I was not. Lots of other people were seeing similar things. Here are just a few:

Take a look at this genuinely eye-opening article from Ipsos.com. *"The world runs on data. Here's how to get people to trust your company with it."* https://www.ipsos.com/en-us/knowledge/society/The-world-runs-on-data. *"Throughout COVID-19, there has been a 400% increase in video conference application downloads."*

"Too often these leaders think they can apply whatever works for them in their face - to - face meetings." (Fraidenburg, M., 2020, p. 28)

"To me, the challenge with on-line meetings is making them more like in person while delivering an equivalent amount of value." Interview with Eric Anderson, COO, Clearwave Corp.

The reasons online meetings are increasing daily are:

Technology has advanced to where we can connect with others at a distance not just by voice alone but now by video. It has expanded our world such that organizations easily connect across the country and around the globe. Organizations are no longer in just one physical location but are spread out. People who rarely, if ever met, now work with each other. Families disperse geographically yet still stay connected. **Nearly everyone** in the tech-enabled countries, not just businesses, has access to video conferencing using computers, smartphones, and tablets.

The economics of distributed businesses, work teams, and employees now makes sense. It is much easier to make them happen and be profitable.

Traffic started to push us to connect using technology rather than in person. We are getting more and more tired of spending a good portion of our day sitting in traffic. Telecommuting is becoming the norm.

The Covid 19 pandemic opened the flood gates. When we were prevented from meeting face-to-face, we opted to use technology, thinking it was almost as good as meeting in-person. Well, after a few months of this, many people are reporting that online meetings generally suck.

Many of these meetings are not as necessary as one might think. We are beginning to experience "online meeting burnout." (https://www.businessnewsdaily.com/15728-zoom-burnout.html) This burnout is costly.

What Are the Presenting Symptoms?

- Right off the bat is all the technical problems that come up from trying to join the meeting through things going wrong during the meeting.
- Next are all the bloopers that happen to attendees, including weird lighting and camera angles, eye-catching stuff seen in the background, distracting background noise.
- In longer meetings, sore butts.

- We feel less connected to the people in the meeting because:
  - We can't touch each other—shake hands, pat each other on the back, or hug. Check out all the studies done before online meetings that have found how important this is.
  - We can't share the same food—break bread together. When we do this in person, suddenly we are talking, connecting, handing napkins, passing the salt, asking if somebody wants more cookies. When we do these things, we are starting to take care of each other, starting to build relationships, starting to trust. Think about how many meetings take place in restaurants.
  - We see each other on two-dimensional screens where you only see part of each person. Plus, we cannot see everyone at once in large meetings. Body language is tough to read. It is key to communicating surprise, disgust, disagreement, humor, acceptance, attention, and many other emotions.

Thought Experiment 1

Think for a moment about the last meeting you were in *face-to-face*. Think about the people you see and hear. Think about the body language you were picking up, how connected you were to the people who were speaking and those listening. Now think about your last *online* meeting, those small talking-head images on the screen. To what extent do you feel the same level of connection to those people?

- It's harder to ask the person next to you for help. Giving someone help is one way we connect.
- Our attention is *split* between people and technology. In a face-to-face meeting, we just have to show up—it's something familiar we've done all our lives. We don't have to spend time figuring out where the mute button is or how to share a handout.
- When we leave an online meeting, we don't have the same subtle rewarding good feeling that goes with sharing time with others that we do in face-to-face meetings. We don't get a chance to chat with others on the way out the door.

So, is all this actually a problem? Online meetings are certainly better than no meetings at all. Right? We get together. We tell a few stories. We make decisions, plans, worship, learn, etc. It is hard to believe that these "symptoms" are all that important. Do online meetings really suck?

Digging Deeper

Maybe yes, maybe no. "*As Jason Fried, co-founder and CEO of Base-camp, once wrote: 'If you're going to schedule a meeting that lasts one hour and invite 10 people to attend then it's a ten-hour meeting, not a one-hour meeting.'*" (Osman, Hassan., 2020, p. 13).

To get started, we need a little background to know what we are looking for.

Our primal need to connect and belong

There seems to be a powerful human need to connect with others. From the time we are born, we crave to be accepted, respected, and loved by others. We are designed to live and function in groups. We are social creatures. We seem to be driven to be part of a family, a class, a group, a neighborhood, an organization, a community. We long to belong (Adlerian psychology). It is so deep-rooted, so primal, that it seems to be built into our genetic make-up.

Further, the bond is not just one way. Think about the deep feelings of satisfaction you get when you accept, respect, help, and love others outside your immediate family. That feeling is deep inside, at the core of our being.

Maslow suggested in his famous hierarchy of needs that the most basic needs were: 1) survival then 2) safety then 3) social. As humans, we understand that survival and safety are much easier to achieve when working with others.

But not just *any* others. They could be a threat. Our immediate reaction when we encounter something or someone new is caution.

Could it be a danger to our survival, safety, or our social connections? We go slowly, cautiously, until we know more and have built a relationship. We don't trust just anyone with our safety and security.

Other emotions like greed and fear get in the way of satisfying this drive to belong. Two thousand years ago, Jesus directed us to "Love one another" over and over again. In Greek translations of the Bible, Jesus used the word "agape" for love when issuing the command. It is a Greek word referring to the highest form of love. He directed us to make this our primary focus—to acknowledge the primal urge to connect and have joy and respect in each other's lives. When

> "A new command I give you: Love one another." John 13:34 NIV
>
> "My command is this: Love each other as I have loved you." John 15:12 NIV
>
> "The second is this: 'Love your neighbor as yourself." Mark 12:31, Luke 10:27, Matthew 22:39 NIV

we do this, the rest (safety, security, social, esteem) will work out (but maybe not without effort). Remember, Jesus was saying this at a time when there were *no online* meetings. People met face-to-face. Most of the deeper connections we make with each other are made by being close to one another, by being there in person. With the advent of online meetings, this has become much more difficult because we are not there in person. I wonder what he would say with today's tech? With the pandemic?

How we connect

When we meet for any reason in-person, we connect in many ways. We get more done working together. It is more rewarding. And while the tasks and results are important, what lies below the surface is even more important—**the connections we make with each other that satisfy the basic human need to belong, to bond with others, to feel secure, to trust each other.** How are those connections made?

- We share doing something together—we share a common experience.

- We share our personal history in small talk between working times. We find we have similar experiences. Indirectly, this small talk communicates our values.
- We share our joys and heartaches.
- We touch each other on the shoulder or shake hands.
- We eat food together, a way to connect that has been with us for eons.
- We communicate interest, surprise, disagreement, humor, acceptance, attention, etc., non-verbally with body language.
- We observe how we behave toward each other.

All these combine to bring us together, allow us to feel close to each other, communicate our values, the things that are important to us, how we look at the world, how we operate and build trust. Trust comes out of strong deep relationships.

Major "Suckitis" cause identified

But wait! We saw in the previous section that much of this is *missing from online meetings.*

> "When you work with an in-person team, there are plenty of opportunities throughout the day to stop, chat, and connect. Those informal conversations and connections help build a rapport that carries over into meetings, making people feel more engaged and perhaps more comfortable voicing their opinions or offering critical feedback. One study found that workers who shared a funny or embarrassing story about themselves with their team produced 26% more ideas in brainstorming sessions than workers who didn't. And the benefits of having a best friend at work have also been well documented." Deanna deBara, January 2nd, 2020, The ultimate guide to remote meetings in 2020, https://slack.com/blog/collaboration/ultimate-guide-remote-meetings

The impact then is lower trust. The bottom line is that it is much harder to share your feelings and values, build a relationship, and build trust if all you do is meet online. It's normally done naturally when we are in each other's physical presence.

Why is trust so important?

The world is changing faster than ever before. It is a race to see who can make things better, smaller, faster, smarter. Is trust losing this race? And if it does, so what?

I think UL, LLC, a global safety certification company, says it best. *"The world runs on trust."* If you do this thought experiment, it won't take you long to see how critically important trust is. If there is no trust, there is no relationship.

Thought Experiment 2

Take a look at the world around you. A serious look. What makes this world possible? What is hidden behind the scenes? What allows people to confidently buy products, use technology, work together, invest, play together, get married, have a family. **Trust**. Imagine for a minute what your world would be like with less trust. (Thanks UL LLC for this inspiration)

Without trust, people are less likely to share and contribute because they don't know what the other person will think of them. We trust others to behave normally in public, not to shoot us, not steal, etc. We trust doctors, medical treatment, legal advice, law enforcement. Almost everything we do when we interact in any way with others involves trust.

Meetings that don't build relationships and trust slowly but surely create more significant problems.

Higher Anxiety: Most of us feel a little more alone, a little more disconnected, a little more anxious because we have not been connecting with our friends as we did before. This is manifesting itself in more racial tension and more political division than we have seen in a long time. In other words, less trust in others.

Fewer Sales: Without trust, things slow down or stop. Just look at how the pandemic has affected our trust. While we still trust other people's expertise, honesty, etc., we don't trust that we are totally safe. We have cut way back on going out to eat, going to church, going to large gatherings, driving (use less gas), having our houses cleaned, going to the movies, shopping in person, trying on clothes, and many other things that involve close contact. Sales are down; businesses are losing money; some have gone under.

Weaker Corporate Culture: Corporate culture is built on trust. Peter Drucker once said, *"Culture eats strategy for breakfast."* I once heard the CEO of a consulting firm say, *"Culture eats planned organizational change for lunch."* Culture is the values and beliefs people share. In some cases, it is learned from experience. In other cases, it is learned from stories told in the break room. Culture in an organization is "how we do things"— how we behave. If people are not in agreement, or even at odds, about how to do things, you're going to get a lot less done.

Today, some businesses are considering having *only* an online presence, no physical location. People would never get together because there is no office. Employees would be hard-pressed to align themselves with the corporate culture if there was one. Can you imagine if you were to join a business like this, how hard it would be to feel like you were part of the company? To feel connected? How strong do you think your loyalty would be? *"Relationships sustain organizations—period."* (Eric Anderson, COO, Clearwave Corp.)

Lower Productivity: From a psychological perspective, groups go through three classic stages: forming, storming, and norming before they get to performing. As we have seen, meeting online makes it more challenging to build relationships and trust. This slows down groups/teams getting through the first three stages. The result is that it takes longer to get to the performing stage. And even when they do, they likely don't perform as well.

Graphically, it looks like this.

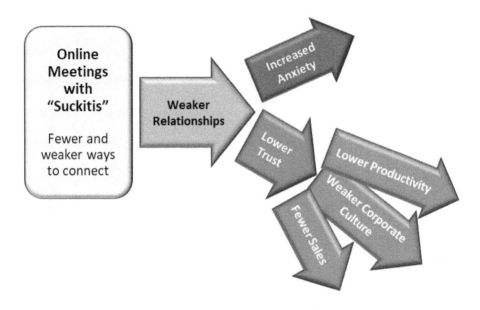

Figure 2: Impact of Weak Relationships and Low Trust

OK, OK. I agree that there is more to building relationships and trust than just meetings. For now, we're going to *think globally and act locally*. For now, our locality is the online meeting where we see symptoms, and we can do something to correct the situation. And, realistically, almost all of any relationship is built when the people involved meet!

What *Can* We Do to Help This Patient?

How can we make online meetings better? How can we make them suck less? How can we come up with a workable, effective treatment plan?

1. First, **analyze** today's online meetings to better understand their limitations, find problem areas, and determine how they differ from in-person meetings. Arrive at a diagnosis.

2. Armed with that information plus a set of driving principles, **plan** online meetings to account for their shortcomings—building

in ways to create and strengthen relationships and trust, make them run smoother, and be less taxing to our brains and back-sides—design them to be "Suck-free." (Treatment Plan Part I)

3. Then, **run** those meetings in ways that take into account the lack of physical presence. (Treatment Plan Part II)

4. And finally, **follow through** and make your next meetings even better. (Treatment Plan Part III)

Let's move on now and take a closer look at the causes of "Suckitis."

Chapter 2

Exactly What Is Wrong with Online Meetings?

"Why do we need to mess around with all these details? Just tell me how to do a better job of planning a meeting." Well, the answer is simple. *"Prescription without diagnosis is malpractice."* Just taking medicine at random has a small chance of fixing a disease. While we have seen the symptoms and the impact if nothing is done, we need a better understanding of what's wrong before designing a treatment plan.

This chapter will give you the knowledge to better understand what's wrong with online meetings today and why they have "Suckitis" to a greater or lesser degree. Once you know what's wrong, you can start fixing yours.

Much of what you will read in this chapter will be no surprise. If you were to see these items on a multiple-choice quiz asking if they were typical of an online meeting, you would get most of them. **In other words, you already know this stuff, but you just haven't thought about it in this way.** Let's get started.

In the case of meetings, most of us have been in many meetings over the years, from classrooms to business meetings to parties to worship services to association meetings to who knows what else. Far fewer people have designed a meeting, and far far fewer have ever learned how to design an *effective* meeting.

To make matters a bit more complicated, we are blazing new trails today. For hundreds of years, we met face-to-face. There's a mountain of material out there on how to have effective face-to-face meetings. Technology has enabled, and now the Covid pandemic, traffic, and convenience have pressured most face-to-face meetings to become virtual. Online meetings have added a new set of issues and limitations most of us are not familiar with, maybe not even aware of, much less how best to deal with them.

Online meetings are better than nothing, but they are a lot like watching a movie—it is not the real thing. There are things partially or totally missing.

Online meetings are not simple. Look at all these parts shown below! And I will bet I have missed a few. How do they all work together?

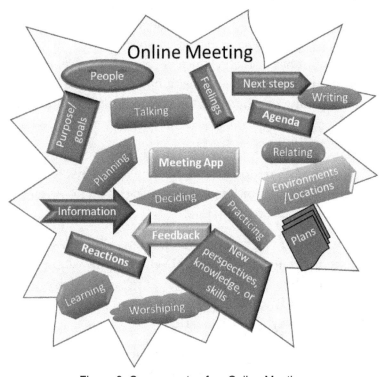

Figure 3: Components of an Online Meeting

Before you can design something that works well, you need a solid understanding of what you are designing. You need more than just a few tips from the internet. You need to know what it is for, what it is supposed to do, what it is made up of, and the principles that govern how it works. Many people know what a house is, what goes into it, and how it works. But few can design a good house. **I want you to be one of those who can plan and run an effective online meeting—a meeting that doesn't suck!**

This chapter will analyze a meeting and give you a simple, useful way of looking at it—a model to help diagnose online meetings. It will take an in-depth look at how an online meeting is different from an in-person one and the problems these differences create. That diagnosis will lead us to our treatment plan.

A Useful Diagnostic Model

When performing a diagnosis, a model of how to proceed comes in very handy. We need a solid framework for designing and running online meetings. Without some kind of model or framework, it is not easy to see how the parts fit together and interact. The one we will use is a simple model of a system.

Wait, don't go! You don't need a Systems Engineering degree to understand it. It is plain talk. It is an easy way to look at meetings so we can perform a complete and thorough diagnosis.

Components of a System

Let's start with a familiar system most of us have in our homes, our house heating system, so we can see we already understand systems. We just need a little better terminology.

- Coming in is fuel, electricity, room temperature, and the settings. These are called "inputs."
- The thermostat uses those to determine what it needs to do to maintain the room temperature. It may send a signal to your furnace to come on and blow some warm air.
- The furnace and ductwork make up the "structure" of the system.

- The heating, cooling, and circulating are "processes."
- Warm air or cool air are the "outputs."
- The thermostat gets "feedback" by checking the room temperature.

Here is how it looks graphically.

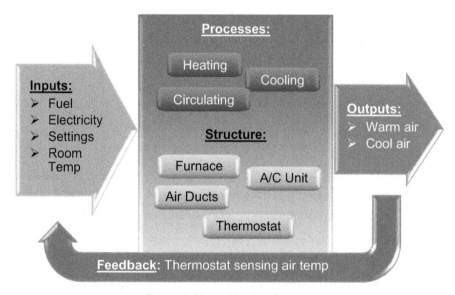

Figure 4: Home Heating System

So, what does an online meeting look like when viewed as a system. Here are all those meeting parts we saw earlier when viewed as a system. They are organized and make a lot more sense.

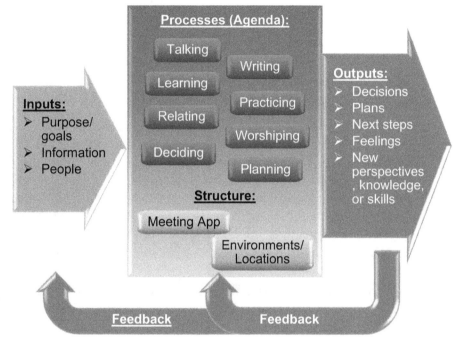

Figure 5: Online Meeting Viewed as a System

Does This Model Apply to My Meeting?

Legitimate question. Let's look at some typical types of meetings.

- **Problem-solving/decision-making** meetings where a few people are working together on something. Everyone is contributing.
- **Information sharing** meetings where the goals are for the attendees to acquire new knowledge or skills. These include small training meetings as well as large conferences with many speakers. In some cases, the intent is for the attendees to retain the information for a long time. In others, like status meetings, it is merely to review the information and see if it affects current activities.
- **Social** meetings where people are getting to know or catching up with each other for purely social/friendship reasons.

- **Experience something** meetings where the goal is for the attendees to sit in on something like a worship service or be entertained with a video via a Facebook link. These usually limit attendee interaction to chat and do not support them being seen or heard.

Are these really systems?

- They all have a **purpose**, stated, and unstated. Some have clear **goals**; others have fuzzy goals.
- Most have **inputs** of people and information.
- The agenda effectively specifies what happens in the meeting—the **processes**. Some have an agenda; others do not. This varies depending on the purpose of the meeting. Many business meetings include making decisions, planning, giving status reports. Training meetings are more focused on learning and practicing. Social meetings are more focused on sharing knowledge, building relationships, and sharing feelings. (I am not going to try to describe worship meetings because someone will justifiably correct me ☺.)
- The **structure** in all these online meetings includes the technology and the environment at the locations of all the attendees and the host or presenter.
- They have different **outputs** depending on the meeting—decisions, plans, next steps, new knowledge or skills, and feelings.
- **Sometimes feedback** is harder to identify. In volunteer environments, people just don't show up again if they didn't get what they wanted. Tough feedback. For all meetings, you can ask people to fill out forms and hope that they will.

The bottom line is the systems model will work for our purposes.

What Is Different About Meeting Online?

⚠️ Warning 1: **Too many people try to conduct their online meetings the same way as they did the face-to-face ones. They try to cram a physical meeting model into a virtual environment. It's like putting on someone else's clothes. They sort of fit but are too big in some places and too small in others.**

For meetings, some things still work as in face-to-face meeting, but many others don't.

Let's use our system model of a meeting to examine the components of a meeting and find out in detail how online is not the same as face-to-face. This will get us ready to design (plan) an effective online meeting and address these differences.

Input Differences

Purpose, Goals

For the most part, these are similar to face-to-face meetings, except that it is even more critical that they are clear so you can keep the meeting focused. Getting off track in an online meeting seems to be more wearing on people than in a face-to-face meeting.

People

Difference 1: You will probably have the same local people at the meeting. With the ability to have people who are distant, you are more likely to have scheduling problems because of personal schedules or different time zones.

Difference 2: Since people in these meetings are now more likely to be spread out geographically, they are less likely to have met each other, known each other in-person before the meeting. They are less likely to have any shared history, such as working for the same boss, meeting in the same church, etc.

Information

Difference 3: Online you have to depend on people receiving and printing or viewing the handouts, including the agenda. You may have sent the handouts to them, but they may not have the handouts at meeting time for a wide variety of reasons.

Process Differences

Talking/Presenting

There are some subtle differences from in-person meetings.

Difference 4: It is harder for someone to be recognized when they want to speak. There are no body language cues available.

Difference 5: The meeting leader must do more to make sure everyone gets to speak.

Difference 6: Face-to-face people would do something to let the speaker know they agree or disagree, like nod their head. Online, because they are not physically in the same room, people do that less.

> A famous study from the 1970s suggested that communication is 7% verbal (what you say), 38% voice tone (the way you say it), and 55% body language. The small pictures of audience members limit what you see and drastically limit what is communicated.

Difference 7: In-person you read the audience and adjust what you're saying and how you say it accordingly. You work with the audience. But online, the first thing you do is mute. Now you can't hear the subtle "yeses" and "uh huhs." You have little body language to read. You can't read the energy in the room. The result is you make fewer adjustments and are a little less effective.

Difference 8: The speaker image frequently occupies a significant portion of the screen. If everyone is not muted, and someone sneezes or blows their nose, they suddenly become the center of attention rather than being ignored, as would happen in a face-to-face meeting.

Writing

Difference 9: Whiteboards, etc.: In face-to-face meetings, presenters can write on whiteboards and flip charts. Participants can write on them too. Online you can do this only to a limited extent. Not all participants will understand how to use the meeting app whiteboard. It takes more computer savvy for the presenter to save and then distribute the whiteboard after the meeting.

Difference 10: Whiteboards again: Another aspect is that it takes up most of the screen when the whiteboard is showing. As a result, participants see it and *not* the other participants or the presenter. In a face-to-face meeting, you could see the whiteboard plus still see the presenter *and* other people in the room.

Difference 11: Note-taking: In face-to-face meetings, participants can take notes easily using pen and paper or laptops. However, in online meetings, the pen and paper are off to the side, not directly in front of the person. The computer is in use by the meeting. (Yes, I know you could split the screen and type notes into a word processor document, but this is beyond many participants. Plus, it would further limit who you could see.)

Deciding, Planning

It is pretty much the same other than hard to see if all agree based on body language (which we have already covered).

Learning, Practicing (Training)

Difference 12: Again, body language. As a presenter, it is hard to read the blank stares indicating people are not getting the point.

Difference 13: Presenters in person seem to project more energy compared to online, even far away like in an arena.

Difference 14: Attention spans are likely shorter due to more distractions and working in a home environment rather than the office.

Worshiping

Most worship services and meetings have gone online during the pandemic. While we cover the social aspects of this elsewhere, a couple of things are different for worshiping online.

Difference 15: For one, worship venues like churches and temples are designed to minimize distractions of all kinds, *and* they abound with religious icons, statues, and images.

Difference 16: For denominations that have Holy Communion, there is no direct sharing of the bread and wine.

Difference 17: For those who laid hands on others during prayer (hands-on healing), that piece of the pie is not possible.

Difference 18: And while you can listen to music online, you cannot sing along together hearing the other people sing due to the slight delays going over the wire or airwaves.

The bright side is now many people who wanted to attend worship services or get individual prayer but could not travel now can at least attend a virtual version of these services or get personal prayer from someone.

> *"Many have found a spiritual connection through TV preachers and now through live streaming of religious services, and we need to celebrate that. However, there are those of us who find our spiritual connection with God renewed and strengthened through communal worship; singing, actively sharing in the prayers and responses with others, and the fellowship found in gathering. Online broadcasts of rituals cannot duplicate the human emotions of love and joy that abound in community."*
> (Personal email from Ed Fuller, a deacon in the Episcopal church)

Hidden Processes

Difference 19: Reading Body Language: Remember, 55% of what is communicated is done via body language. It is much more difficult due to the small screens and the fact that most people are sitting. There is less body language because less of the body is involved, less of the body moving around. There is no time when people are standing around together.

Difference 20: Building Personal Relationships & Trust: Online, these one-on-one connections are much more difficult. In addition to making a direct connection with others, a good portion of relationship building comes from observing how people interact and treat each other. Since there is less to *observe* due to fewer opportunities and technology limits, there is not as much information for us to use to build relationships.

Face-to-face	Online
Participants relate during breaks. People connect one-on-one.	**Difference 21:** Body language is much harder to read online, not just by the presenter or leader, but by the participants.
They read body language, either consciously or unconsciously.	**Difference 22:** You can't shake hands or give someone a hug or pat on the back.
They watch how people treat others.	**Difference 23:** People can't just walk up to someone and strike up a conversation getting to know strangers or catching up with friends.
They gain rapport. They build interpersonal trust.	**Difference 24:** There are fewer opportunities, and it is harder to see how people treat each other.

People end up forming surface impressions of others rather than more profound relationships.

Difference 25: Getting Help—Questions/Directions: When people have questions like, "Where are we?", they can ask the person next to them in face-to-face meetings without interrupting the speaker. Online, they are locked into waiting till the speaker is finished. The result may be frustration or missing the point the speaker is making.

Agenda

Difference 26: Time Zones: Online meetings frequently span time zones. Now you have to be sure the time of day works for all attendees, plus you have to make doubly sure that people know what time zone you are referring to when you announce the meeting—3:00 Eastern, 2:00 Central.

Difference 27: Meeting Duration: People can't sit in one place locked into staring at a screen and keep focused for hours. Breaks become critical.

Difference 28: Variety: For the same reason, more variety is needed in online meetings than in face-to-face ones.

Difference 29: Evening Meetings: I have seen a tendency to have evening meetings. There is energy when people meet together outside the home that keeps them awake well past their regular bedtime. People often attend online evening meetings from home—the bedtime environment. This can lead to people tiring more quickly in evening meetings than in daytime meetings.

Structure Differences

Structure is what is needed to support the process is in the meeting.

Meeting Application

Difference 30: Now people have to be at least a little familiar with the meeting app being used. Face-to-face all people had to do was show up in the meeting room. Now there are lots of settings to deal with in the meeting app. Security. We have to learn how to do new things like showing a video online. Some require a lot of your attention.

- Breakout sessions in-person go like this: "Okay, now go to breakout stations and …"
- Online, someone has set up breakout rooms and assign people to them. They have to do this *while* the meeting is running. Then they have to open the breakout rooms. All this requires focused attention.

Today I am part of a team planning an online celebration or party for a small church. In addition to the usual publicity, agenda planning, and rehearsals, we have to set up quite a few "app training sessions." These will ensure that all the people who might attend are on the right level Zoom and know how to do basic things such as go in and out of breakout rooms and change their view.

Environments

And it is not just more tech; it is tech that is no longer mostly under the control of the meeting host. (This is not to say that face-to-face meetings don't have their share of tech problems. We all have seen them.)

 Warning 2: Online meetings are much more complicated than they appear. Because there are so many moving parts, most of which are out of your control, there is a much higher probability of technical problems. Test. Practice. Test. Try out. Train. Test.

Difference 31: Online, each person attending is responsible for part of the technology that makes the meeting happen, enough to get connected and maybe see and print handouts. People have different devices (computers, tablets, smartphones), routers, modems, internet providers, etc. There are many more working parts. Consider a 10-person meeting. There are 10 email apps, 10 meeting apps like Zoom, 10 devices, 10 cameras, 10 microphones, 10 speakers, 10 keyboards, 10 cursor control methods (mouse, touchpad, touch screen), 10 routers, and 10 internet connections. So now you are looking at **100** working parts instead of just 10! They all must work correctly to have a smooth meeting.

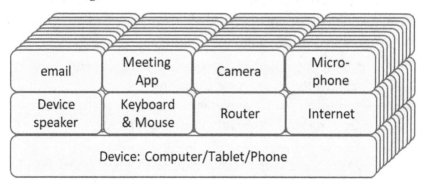

Figure 6: 100 Working Parts - One Set of Components/Person

In face-to-face meetings, if you have a problem, lots of times you can get someone to come in and fix it. Now you potentially have people with technology problems far away. No technician is available (the teenager is at a party).

All this leads to people coming to the meeting late or frustrated because they had difficulty finding the invitation, connecting, etc.

Face-to-face meetings are held in offices, small meeting rooms, or large hotel conference rooms. Most venues have been designed to have a physical environment conducive to meetings. They have appropriate lighting and seating. They have been designed to minimize distractions. Online there are *many* venues, one for each person who is attending. For the most part, they have *not* been designed specifically for meetings. They are less business/work-oriented. Multiple environments come into play instead of just one. Unlike in-person meeting environments, these are not so easily controlled or meeting-friendly, as we shall see.

Difference 32: Lighting: It turns out that getting good lighting while sitting in front of your computer is not so easy. It may require that you add lighting in front of you, decrease lighting coming from behind you, or even get some additional software for your computer to adjust brightness, contrast, and color.

Difference 33: Seating: For short meetings, whatever seating is available is likely fine, but for longer meetings like day-long conferences, comfortable seating becomes essential. Commercial or business settings either have comfortable seating, or the people end up moving around so their butt does not get too sore.

Difference 34: Body Position: In online meetings, participants are kind of locked into sitting in a chair facing in one direction, the screen. Their unconscious movement is severely restricted. In face-to-face meetings, there is frequently body movement:

- People move their heads as the speaker moves about the room or simply turning to look at other participants or the various flipcharts on the wall.
- People are changing rooms between sessions.

- People are up and about writing on the flipchart.
- People may move around the room for a quick breakout session at another table.
- People may get up to get coffee from the pot in the same room.

In online meetings, these things are not done.

Now body position may not seem like a big deal, but it is, especially in long meetings. **The body needs this movement so the mind can stay focused.**

Difference 35: Camera Angle: In face-to-face meetings, everyone is usually sitting except maybe the person currently presenting. You see everyone from a normally expected viewing angle. This is *not* true in online meetings because of where the cameras are. People use different devices or have their device in a comfortable place. The result is that the camera gives an unusual view of participants or, worse yet, the presenter. You end up thinking about how odd they look instead of what they are saying. Just think about all the strange views you have seen.

Difference 36: Casual Dress: Because people are at home, they tend to dress more casually. Outside-the-home dress brings a bit more formality and focus when people gather.

Difference 37: Refreshments: Home computer environments are usually not designed to have refreshments like coffee or water in the meeting room. The result is that if someone wants a cup of coffee, they have to leave the meeting instead of just going over to the coffee pot.

Difference 38: Distractions: The usual home venue is usually not designed to control distractions. There may be children, unwanted spouses, distracting lighting, background objects (statues, fans, …), barking dogs, or even loud teenage music.

Difference 39: Device Screen: For most people, everything is smaller than real life, tiny if they are on a smartphone! Plus, these are only two-dimensional. So what? The presenter and other participants' impact is much less on the person viewing—another reason why there is less body language communicated.

Difference 40: Device Screen: Another limitation of the device screen in larger meetings is that you cannot see everyone at one time. Remember the last time you were in a big meeting? You could look all around the room and see everyone there. You could feel the energy in the room. You can't do that online. You can only see one screen full of pictures at a time. Try that on a smartphone!

Difference 41: Not the Same Space: There is something about meeting in one place that brings people together. You're sharing the same physical space in a meeting room. That is certainly not the case online where everyone is in a different location. Some of the commonality, connecting is lost.

Difference 42: Behaving Differently: When we meet in a meeting room, we behave differently than we do in our homes. Our homes are much more casual and safer environments. Sometimes this affects productivity and staying on track. We are more relaxed and more likely to get off track and talk about non-meeting-related topics.

> **Experience may be the best teacher, but …**
>
> I just attended a meeting where one of the five people in the meeting was in his comfortable office at home. He rotated in his chair back and forth during the whole meeting. I spent much of my time watching him instead of staying focused on the meeting content.

Outcome Differences

Decisions, Plans, Next Steps

I don't see a lot of difference in how you make decisions or plans between online and face-to-face. If there is, it's not very obvious.

Feelings

Difference 43: For the most part, in most all meetings, these are hidden outcomes, and in many cases, may go completely unnoticed.

People leave meetings with feelings about how it was run, what other people said or did, and what results were achieved. Much of the time, people are not aware of these unless something was particularly good or bad. The intensity of these feelings is generally less in online meetings due to the lack of physical presence *and how* people convey their feelings about the topics. As we saw earlier, research has shown that more than half of communication is in body language. So, feelings are not as well communicated, which in turn limits the extent to which people build relationships.

Learning: New Knowledge, Skills, or Ways of Thinking About Something

The jury is still out on this one. I could not find much research or even articles to indicate there is a significant difference in how well things are learned. If you know of any, please let me know for the next edition.

Difference 44: One small limitation is that it's not relatively as easy to ask questions of the instructor. There are ways to raise your hand using technology, but it's still not as easy as sticking your arm up in the air. So, people may be a little bit more reluctant to ask questions or at least ask fewer questions than they did face-to-face

Feedback Differences

Face-to-Face	Online
You can hand out formal meeting evaluations, and most people will fill them out before they leave.	**Difference 45:** You can't physically hand out anything. People can leave the meeting without completing the evaluation form. You email the formal evaluations and hope people will return them.

Face-to-Face	Online
The filled-out forms do not require any form of identification.	**Difference 46:** If you use email, the most common method for getting feedback, then individual feedback is no longer anonymous.
You can get informal feedback from people at breaks and afterward in the office.	**Difference 47:** You don't get a chance to meet people face-to-face casually and get informal feedback. The result is less feedback, even when asked.

Diagnosis from Analysis

Using the systems model to analyze an online meeting and examine the differences should have convinced you that trying to put a physical meeting into a virtual one is like putting a round peg in a square hole. Our diagnosis shows us that there are many areas where we can minimize "Suckitis" by:

- maximizing those things that people like to get out of a meeting but aren't right now and
- minimizing those things that frustrate people and detract from the meeting's effectiveness.

From Diagnosis to Treatment Plan

Well, what do you think now? Does it sound like some of this stuff fits the meetings you've attended? Hopefully, you now realize there are many subtle differences, significant differences, between online meetings and face-to-face ones. It sure looks our diagnosis is that our patient, online meetings, has "Suckitis." Now we are *almost* ready to develop a treatment plan. We need some principles to base our treatment plan on.

PART 2: TREATMENT PLAN

Out treatment plan consists of some basic principles that define cause and effect, plus some guidelines and best practices for putting those principles into action.

Driving Principle	Action Guidelines
1. **Engagement:** When people are not engaged in the meeting, outcomes will suffer.	Keep people engaged.
2. **Relationships:** When people connect, trust, productivity, and satisfaction go up while anxiety goes down.	Plan for ways to help people connect and build relationships and trust.
3. **What Gets Rewarded:** What gets rewarded gets repeated.	Plan for deliverables. Summarize accomplishments and thank people for participating.
4. **People Support What They Create**: Not what you dictate.	Get people to participate. Highlight how people contributed.
5. **Information Overload:** If people are given too much information at one time, they are unlikely to remember any of it.	Limit new information to bite-sized chunks.
6. **Wasting Time:** When people feel their time is being wasted, they become disengaged in the meeting.	Have a clear purpose and objectives. Prepare for your meetings, stay on track, eliminate technical problems.

Driving Principle	Action Guidelines
7. **Distractions:** People tend to focus on distractions instead of the meeting. They disengage in the meeting.	Minimize distractions as much as possible. Keep meetings to a reasonable length, incorporate breaks.
8. **Follow-Up:** Meeting follow-up improves productivity, satisfaction, and future meetings.	Get feedback, give feedback, so you continue to improve

Our diagnosis tells us that these guidelines need to focus mostly on two components of an online meeting: the processes and the structure. And because we are still learning about online meetings, feedback is even more essential to help have better future meetings.

We will apply these guidelines to each of the three stages of delivering a meeting to develop a three-part treatment plan based on a meeting's components.

   I. Changes to Designing/planning a meeting

  II. Changes to Running a meeting

 III. Changes to Following-up after the meeting

Chapter 3

Treatment I: Plan "Suck-free" Online Meetings in 8 Easy Steps

If you ran meetings before the online wave, you probably already did some version of the things covered in this chapter. You probably did many of them automatically without even thinking about them. For the online meeting, you just need to think about things a little bit differently and attend to a few more details that are not there in face-to-face meetings. This chapter will guide you in doing that.

In the last chapter, we used the systems model to analyze online meetings to identify the differences between face-to-face and online meetings. Now we are ready to use that model to help us prescribe ways to alleviate and maybe even cure some of the symptoms by planning a great online meeting. One of the keys will be balancing getting the work done with building relationships.

 Best Practice 1: Don't just slap an agenda together. Spend time designing/planning your online meeting, especially the first one. *"If you want people to come back, make the first meeting 'standing ovation good.'"* **Sharon Pitman**

How Does One *Design* a Meeting?

Since we are using the systems model to analyze and treat our meetings, the question becomes, "how does one design a system?" Systems don't just appear; they are created to satisfy a need, for some reason or purpose. (To be clear, here we are talking about human systems that are created for a purpose, not about human systems that evolve like societies or systems in nature like a storm system.) Here is a high-level road map for an online meeting as a system.

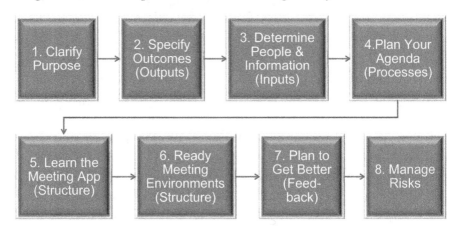

Figure 7: The Process of Building a System

It goes like this:

1. First, clarify why you need the system, what it is for, its purpose.
2. Next, nail down the desired outputs or outcomes of the meeting.
3. Then round up the inputs needed to create those outputs.
4. Knowing these, figure out what you need to do (processes) to transform those inputs into the desired outputs.
5. Determine the structure those processes require. The meeting app is one.
6. Meeting environments is the other.
7. Get feedback to keep this system on track and make it better.
8. And if you have a complex system, a long, complicated meeting, manage the risks.

As we work through the details of the treatment plan, you will see references to these principles. These principles are put into action with the guidelines.

On the next page is an easy checklist that comes out of these eight steps. Once you've read through these eight steps, you'll be able to do most of your work with just the checklist. If you forget something, simply reread that step.

Checklist for Planning a "Suckfree" Online Meeting

From Steps 1: Purpose, 2: Outcomes, 3: People & Information
- ☐ Have a clear purpose
- ☐ Framed meeting outcomes as deliverables
- ☐ Pre-meeting information sent out and receipt verified

From Step 4: Agenda
- ☐ Written a meeting leader version of the agenda
- ☐ Made time of day clear
- ☐ Included ideas to increase engagement
- ☐ Included ways to build relationships and trust
- ☐ Refined for the specific type of meeting: task or social, working or information, repetitive or one time, short or long, new faces or familiar faces, learning,
- ☐ Have more roles as needed (i.e. Tech Support)

From Step 5: App Features/Technology
- ☐ Configured a strong, reliable Internet connection
- ☐ Have practiced using a waiting room
- ☐ Ready to use breakout rooms
- ☐ Prepared for recording the meeting
- ☐ Prepared for taking screenshots
- ☐ Prepared for conducting polls
- ☐ Practiced sharing documents and using online whiteboards
- ☐ Practiced playing music or videos
- ☐ Practiced muting everyone

From Step 6: Environments
- ☐ Have your presenter's notes ready
- ☐ Your "meeting room" looks professional or at least free from distractions
- ☐ Refreshments for long meetings
- ☐ A good chair
- ☐ A good camera angle
- ☐ Good lighting
- ☐ Have alerted attendees how to upgrade their environments

From Step 7: Plan to Get Better
- ☐ Have feedback questions ready
- ☐ Feedback email is ready to send

From Step 8: Manage Risks
- ☐ For important meetings, risk analysis is complete
- ☐ Backup plans and people are in place

Step 1: Clarify the Meeting's Purpose

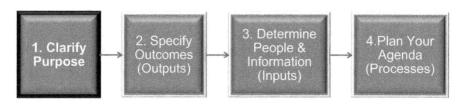

There is nothing significantly different about this step and the next when you compare online meetings to in-person meetings. When researching material for this book, I found plenty of information on meeting outcomes (goals, objectives) but extraordinarily little on what drives those, the meeting purpose. That was amazing, considering that it is critical to a meaningful meeting.

> **Driving Principles:** 3. What gets rewarded, 6. Wasting time

So, let's begin by getting clear about why you are having this meeting. What is the reason you are having this meeting? Once we have this, we make it more concrete with goals/objectives—the meeting outcomes. Having these will give focus to your meeting. They will help keep you from wasting participants' time and, most importantly, provide the participants with a feeling of accomplishment at the end of the meeting.

The meeting purpose may be clear or fuzzy. Lots of times, fuzzy is fine, especially for casual, informal meetings. That is not so true for more formal meetings, meetings that are set up to accomplish something.

 Warning 3: **When the meeting purpose is not clear, well ...**

★ If you don't know where you are going, you will end up somewhere else. (Yogi Berra)

★ If you don't know where you are going, any road will take you there.

★ If you don't know where you are going, how will you know when you have arrived?

Every meeting has at least one purpose, sometimes more. People are meeting to get something done. And this purpose drives pretty much everything else: the goals, agenda, who attends, the technology, what information is shared, what happens during the meeting (the processes), the meeting outcomes, and where and when the meeting happens. Why are you having this meeting? What long-term impact is this meeting intended to have?

- To get the new product to market
- To increase sales
- To increase our spirituality
- To increase connectedness

Guideline 1: **Get clear about the purpose of your meeting. Write it down. Clarity leads to success.**

Now let's use this to determine *precisely* what we want to get out of this meeting—what we want people to walk away with.

Step 2: Make Meeting Outcomes Perfectly Clear

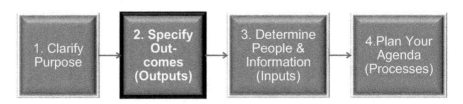

There is not much difference between online and in-person meeting outcomes, but I want to give it a page or two because it is crucial plus including an important tip. Having clear outcomes will make it easier for you as a facilitator to keep the meeting on track—a critical factor in online meetings. It will also help the attendees get a sense of accomplishment.

> **Driving Principles:** 3. What Gets Rewarded, 6. Wasting time

Meeting goals/objectives are simply a way of crystallizing the meeting purpose to be more observable and maybe measurable. (I use goals and objectives as synonyms in this book.) There are lots of books and articles about how to write clear goals, so no point in rehashing that here. Just answer these questions. "What will success look like?" "What do you hope to get out of the meeting?" "What specifically are you trying to accomplish?"

The more formal, the more important the meeting, the more time you should spend clarifying what you want to happen as a result of the meeting. Try to get specific but leave room for creativity and innovation.

- What decisions or plans are you looking for?
- What new knowledge, skills, or ways of thinking about something (perspective or attitude) do you want people to acquire?
- How do you hope they will feel about the meeting itself and the outcomes?
- What will success look like?

 Warning 4: Beware of fuzzy goals. You'll end up spending lots of time but not getting meaningful results. Change your goals to "deliverables."

Confession: When I first wrote this section, I fell into the same trap many people do regarding goals or objectives. I wrote a couple of them this way:

- Our goal is to learn how to …
- Our goal for this meeting is for you to learn the features of the new product so you can better sell it.
- Our goal is to brainstorm ideas for ….

The problem with these objectives is that they are a little fuzzy. It can be quite hard to tell if they have been achieved or not. So, after talking with a senior exec friend of mine, I decided to switch terms. **Goals and objectives may be sufficient for strategic planning, but**

the term "deliverable" is considerably more concrete for a meeting. A deliverable is something specific. Most of the time, you can point to it or do something to be sure it is there. **So, the bottom line is to state your desired outcomes in terms of** *deliverables.*

You can think of the **purpose** as a higher-level goal. Then the **deliverables** (desired outcomes/goals/objectives) get specific about *how* you will achieve the purpose. Here are a few examples using the purposes we listed earlier:

Purpose	Outcomes ➜ Deliverables
To get the new product to market	At least three ways to solve a production problem
	Selected which company to use for raw materials to make the product
	A plan for the coming week/month/year
To increase sales	Attendees can list all the new features of the new product
	Sales reps demonstrate they can use the Star-Man sales technique
To increase our spirituality	Be able to explain how scripture ___ applies to ___.
	To pray together or for one another
To increase connectedness	Have fun
	Shared experiences
	Play trivia

Guideline 2: Have clear deliverables (objectives) for your meeting. This will help you keep the meeting on track during the meeting. When it starts down a rabbit hole, you can get it back on track by referring to these deliverables. These also give you something concrete to judge the effectiveness of the meeting after it is over.

A Word About Status Meetings

Status meetings are some of the most boring meetings out there. Mostly they are information-sharing meetings, which may be better summarized and sent out in an email. If you are to run one of these, get clear exactly why people have to recount what they have done. Why do others need to know all this stuff? Once you have that down, see if you can trim the reports down to the essence and provide detail in other documents. From my experience, there are two goals in status meetings.

- Recognize accomplishments (to motivate people) (Note that this one is tough to make a "deliverable.")
- Make people aware of something happening in one area may affect or be useful to another. The deliverable becomes a list of changes based on reports—a to-do list.

Hearing that the sales dept. is doing well may be useful to hear by the people in production, so they know their jobs are safe and what they are doing is worthwhile. Hearing that the new product development has hit a roadblock may keep sales from selling too much too soon. So, have the people reporting focus on information that could affect other areas. If you continually get nothing in your reports, maybe these reports are not needed. (More on how to handle status meetings when we talk about the agenda a little later.)

Step 3: Decide *Who* Should Attend and *What* Information Is Needed

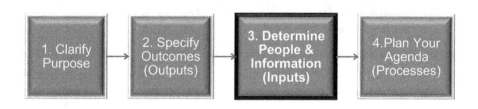

Who do you need to have in the meeting to create your deliverables?

> Driving Principle: 6. Wasting time

For the most part, this is the same as any in-person meeting. Simply invite only the people who need to be there.

 Warning 5: Do not invite people who do *not* have an *active* part in a working meeting to the meeting.

Have a separate meeting for people who need the information but are not part of the decisions or planning. The agenda and presentation in the information-sharing meetings will look different than in a working meeting.

? Common Problems and How to Solve Them

Common Problem 1: Unprepared Presenter: Check with the presenters by phone to be sure they are ready. If a presenter has never done this before, have a short practice session. Speaking online is a bit different than standing in front of a podium. I have seen one presenter continually put his notes on his laptop keyboard. No big deal except that every time he moved them, the laptop microphone picked up the loud rustling.

Common Problem 2: Long-winded people: Be prepared to cut them off and get other people talking politely. If the same person monopolizes every meeting, record in one meeting with a stopwatch (on your phone) how long they talk. Is it really out of proportion to everyone else? If so, then call them between meetings and address the issue.

Common Problem 3: People don't know each other very well: There is a need for people to connect and trust each other. Include relationship-building opportunities in your agenda. (See more detail in the next step on Agenda.)

Common Problem 4: Different meeting times due to time zones: People in the meeting are in different time zones. Pay attention to that and make it very clear in the meeting invitation.

What information do people need to have?

> Driving Principles: 6. Wasting time, 8. Information Overload

Again, this is quite similar to face-to-face meetings. Typically, there are two types of information you want to get to the attendees *before* the meeting: the invitation and handouts. In both cases, you have to depend on email or downloading something from a website.

Send the invitation out 2-3 days before the meeting with the handout attachments, if any. Earlier than that, the email stands a good chance of getting lost, and people are likely to put off reading the handouts.

Send the email out again the day of the meeting.

If this is the first meeting for some people, check with them to be sure they received the email and get them to try the link to the meeting.

If the handouts are critical to the meeting, confirm people have received the handouts, can open them, and what is to be done with them before the meeting.

> **Guideline 3: Limit the amount of new information presented at the meeting to something that people can remember. Delivering vast quantities will only result in information overload.**

? Common Problems and How to Solve Them

Common Problem 5: Information overload: Be sure to limit the amount of information presented. Online meetings take more out of the average brain than in-person ones for several reasons.

Common Problem 6: Missing handouts: People did not receive the handouts, or they could not print them. Send handouts out early and make sure people can open and print them.

Common Problem 7: Missing or invalid invitation: Verify that people did receive the invitation and that it does work. Send the invitation out a few days before the meeting and then the day of the meeting. Put it on your website if possible.

Step 4: Write an Online-Specific Agenda

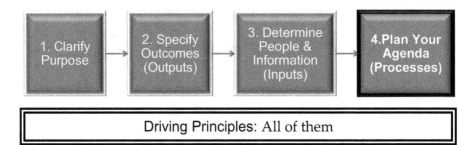

Your agenda specifies what will happen in the meeting—the *processes* you will use in the meeting—your plan for the meeting. You specify who will talk and when, how things will work, breakout sessions, polls, whiteboards, videos, music, etc.

Draft Your Agenda to Achieve the Outcomes

 Best Practice 2: Write an agenda so everyone knows what to expect and help keep the meeting to stay on track.

One useful way to think of your agenda is as a work plan. A typical agenda might look something like this. The most important thing to remember here is that your first draft is very rough. It merely lists the items you want to talk about; it doesn't make sure your meeting will be a success. Including who and how long (time allotted to the topic) will help keep the meeting on track and manage participant expectations.

Figure 8: Sample Agenda with *Notes*

Staff Meeting 10/20/2022 at 11:00 EDT (10:00 CDT, 8:00 PDT)	
Open meeting	
(welcome, intros, ice breakers, check-in)	Everyone—5min
Purpose & Deliverables	Who—How Long
Word these as something you can quickly tell whether or not you achieved them.	
Ground rules and parking lot* as needed	Who—How Long
Identify changes to ___ plan	Who—How Long
Put your most critical topics first. People get burned out more quickly online than in person.	
Finance: What steps to take for deficit?	Who—How Long
Better to frame topics so that the deliverable/outcome is apparent rather than just a topic.	
One useful technique for your topics is to frame them as questions. Instead of "Strategic plan update" write, "What changes do we need to make to the strategic plan?" Instead of "Company picnic," write, "Which company should we use for ___?"	
Next topic	Who—How Long
Each topic should have a clear outcome (deliverable).	
Next topic	Who—How Long
Next topic	Who—How Long
Close meeting	Who—How Long
Include a summary of what you accomplished, next steps, and that you will be asking for feedback.	

* **Parking lot** is a place to record topics or issues during the meeting that are not part of the current agenda. This helps the meeting leader keep the meeting focused on its purpose and deliverables instead of spending valuable time on side issues.

More Casual Meetings: For more casual meetings, you might have another version of the agenda with just the topics listed, knowing that the topics may change in duration. You could replace the word "agenda" with "events," "Topics for Today," or simply list the meeting heading, time, and date, and just list the things you will cover in order.

Status Meetings: EOS Worldwide offers some free tools at https://www.eosworldwide.com/eos-tools that will help make your regular status meetings much more effective. Traction Tools is an online software service that helps organizations facilitate their meetings focusing on using EOS (Entrepreneurial Operating System). https://www.mytractiontools.com.

> **Guideline 4: A good length for short meetings is an hour or less with a maximum of an hour and a half. When people get uncomfortable, they disengage.**

Meeting Time of Day

If your participants are spread across more than one time zone, make sure that people know what time zone you are referring to—3:00 Eastern, 2:00 Central. Put all relevant time zone times in your invitation.

Watch out for scheduling meetings that may interfere with meals or bedtime in other time zones.

> **Guideline 5: Include the time of day for all participant time zones.**

How to Annotate Your Draft Agenda to Increase Success

Here is a way to keep track of the refinements so you remember these ideas *during* the meeting. Then we're going to cover some general ideas to increase engagement and build relationships. These ideas don't necessarily apply to all meetings. A little later, we will cover how to adapt your agenda for different types of meetings like working meetings versus information sharing, regular repeating meetings, issue-based meetings, one-time meetings, and social meetings.

Create a Meeting Leader Version of the Agenda

It is much more important to consciously do things to maintain participant engagement in online meetings than in face-to-face meetings. As you read this section, you will likely make refinements to your draft agenda. Some will be improvements in the wording, sequence, or topics themselves. Other refinements will be ideas on how you will handle the various topics and keep people involved in the meeting.

Sometimes it can be hard to remember all the things you were going to do during the meeting. Create an agenda just for you the same way instructors do. They have the class materials, plus they have "instructor notes." One way is shown in the parts in *italics* in the Sample Agenda above.

Start with your draft agenda and add:

- Ways you will keep people engaged, such as polls, using the "reaction" button, etc.
- Different roles you are going to assign to people during the meeting
- Questions you can ask to keep people engaged
- Notes on additional resources in case you need them
- Reminders to do things or mention specific points

 Best Practice 3: Create meeting leader version of the agenda with notes on how to make it a great meeting.

Now, read on and create your leader version of the agenda.

Ideas to Increase Engagement

Maintaining participant engagement is a critical part of this step.

"Attention is a limited resource. In his famous book, Brain Rules, John Medina presents his Rule # 4: 'We don't pay attention to boring things.' A single activity, like passively listening during an online meeting, quickly becomes boring, Solution: Medina recommends changing gears every ten minutes when making presentations. Otherwise, he says, people's attention will fade away." (Fraidenburg, Michael., 2020, p. 48)

Indeed, this advice applies to in-person meetings. It is even more important in online meetings because it is much easier for participants' attention to wander.

 Warning 6: No matter how good your presentation is, how good your technology is, or how much information you have, you may not end up with your deliverables if people are not engaged. Your meeting may suck. Online it is much harder to keep people engaged than it is in-person.

Guideline 6: Once you have the agenda topics, add ideas on how you will keep people engaged online.

If this is your first time leading an online meeting, this can be daunting. It is better to prepare now than to blow it later. Remember, "Prior Planning Prevents Pee Poor Performance." Here are some of the easy ways you can keep people engaged:

Interactivity

- Facilitate, don't dictate (more on this in the next chapter).
- Use polls (voting).
- Use breakout sessions to divide up into small groups to discuss things or practice and then

Thought Experiment 3

Try this simple relaxation experiment. Get in a quiet place. Then count down from 10 to 1 relaxing a different part of your body with each count without letting your mind wander to somewhere else. Most people find that getting to 1 is hard because their mind has found something else to think about. **Keep people engaged!**

report back to the whole group.

- Get physical - lead people in stretching during breaks.
- Break long topics into sections.
- Break long meetings into several shorter ones.
- Have people use the nonverbal feed-  back features like Reactions and Raise Hand in Zoom.
- Plan your questions to keep people engaged. "Why would ...?", "How would ...?", "Under what circumstances would you ...?", "What do the rest of you think?" "What's next?" "Would you summarize ...?"
- Have more than one presenter during the meeting—have different people present different topics.
- Use online whiteboards or documents that are written on *during* the meetings.

Ideas for Using Breakout Sessions

The typical use for a breakout room is to divide the whole group up and have them work on something in small groups of 3-5 people. That way, more people get to contribute, and people get to know each other better. Then, when the breakout session is over, each group reports to the others. Here are a few ways to use breakout rooms:

- All breakout rooms can work on the same topic.
- Each breakout room can discuss a different topic.
- Another way is to have one or two specialists/experts in each room, and people can go in one at a time and get advice on their particular concern. Spiritual groups can use this to have people with a specific need get individual prayers. To make this work, you will need someone in the main room monitoring when the rooms are available. If you have more people wanting help than experts, you can set up a "waiting" breakout room and put people in there until an expert is available.
- And a straightforward way is to simply put a few people in a breakout room just to get to know each other.

Hack 1: Zoom allows you to let people self-select the breakout room they want to go into. You can name your breakout rooms to be about specific topics then people who want to discuss that topic can join that room.

Ideas for Adding Variety

Think about how professional news shows do this. They don't just have one newscaster talking the whole time. They use several different people. They switch between things showing on the screen: newscaster 1, newscaster 2, photo, video, a newscaster in the middle of the hurricane (why is he taking such a risk?), a reporter on the scene in a riot (again, why is she taking that risk?). You can do the same. (No, not take risks; you can have different people talk.)

- **Have multiple presenters.** Here, I am not talking about getting different people to answer questions or express their opinions. Having several presenters with short segments is more interesting than having just one presenter the whole time (assuming but none of them are particularly boring ☺).

- **Use props.** Instead of something simple like PowerPoint or a Word document, use some 3D props. After watching a couple of presenters use props, I realized they effectively draw attention and make a point. Props will further keep people engaged, and they will better remember what you are saying.

- **Use graphic visuals,** such as photographs, diagrams, charts. Some research has shown that these increase engagement by as much as 94%!

- **Mix it up.** Don't just have the audience see you talking the whole time or PowerPoint slides the entire time. Have them see you for a while, then bullet points in text form, then graphics or photos. If you use text visuals like PowerPoint bullet points, use these sparingly. Do not return to "death by PowerPoint."

- **Add a little music** but keep music segments to 5 minutes or less for the same reasons. See if you can put the lyrics up on the screen while the music is playing.

- **Use videos.**

- **Plan stories** that relate to the topics.

> **Guideline 7:** **Plan a short stretch break every hour. Universities learned this long ago. Instruct the people to get up and maybe even talk them through a stretch or two.**
>
> **Guideline 8:** **The longer the meeting, the more variety you need and the more effort you need to make to get people involved. Use videos, polls, breakout rooms, people contributing to a whiteboard, etc.**

 Pause for a moment and do a quick self-check. How many of these ideas do you think would help you? It will give you an idea of how much difference they can make.

Special Note Regarding New Features or New People

"Train First—Meet Later. If your participants are new to online meeting technology or if your group needs to use sophisticated features of the technology, a lot can go wrong in a hurry just because they are not familiar with the tech system and its features." (Fraidenburg, Michael., 2020, p. 31).

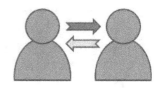 **Warning 7:** **Don't try to solve problems with new technology or new people during a meeting. It wastes everyone's time and annoys the fool out of prepared people.**

Instead, schedule a pre-meeting for new people or to introduce and "train" on a new feature.

Refine Your Agenda to Build Relationships and Trust

As we mentioned earlier, the advent of virtual meetings has made it much more likely that people in these meetings do not know each other. This hidden process of getting to know each other builds trust. People need to trust each other to work together. Refine your agenda to build relationships/foster personal connections.

Warning 8: Online meetings are particularly vulnerable to low trust. Failing to build trust can undermine all your best work.

Here are a few things you can do:

- If you have recurring meetings, start them 15 minutes early and have people drop in and chat. Have some breakout rooms people can go into if they want to get away from the crowd and talk just to each other. They just ask the tech support person to put them in a breakout room so they can talk. By the way, Zoom supports self-select breakout rooms where people can see who is in the breakout rooms and go into anyone they want.

- Where you have recurring meetings with a group that is just getting to know each other, have one or two people give their "how I got here" story each meeting. Limit their stories to around three minutes.

- Include some ice breakers.

- Start meetings off with each person listing one *positive* thing that happened to them this past week or one challenge they are facing.

- If the number of people is reasonable, say 20 or less with little or no prior relationship, and they will be meeting each other several times, consider creating a simple directory with their photo, name, location (maybe just city), reason for being in the meeting, job if relevant, etc. and distribute.

- Use breakout room sessions where the sole purpose is to chat and get to know each other.

- If you are leading a new team that will be working with each other for a long time, schedule some "get to know you" meetings where the whole point is just to learn more about each other and build relationships.

Guideline 9: Plan opportunities to create new or strengthen existing relationships, build trust, and bond as a group or team.

 Warning 9: **Be wary of check-in time.** While negative things are important, they can weigh the meeting down. If you allow people to talk extensively about negative things during check-in, the discussion will tend to go on and on. The person in the problem typically needs to talk to get it

out of their system and work through it. The other people in the meeting frequently try to help the person with the problem. The result is a 30-second check-in ends up taking 10-15 minutes of valuable meeting time and turning some people off. When you sense that someone has a problem and they need to work through it, schedule another meeting to discuss it.

? Pause for a moment and do a quick self-check. How many of these ideas would help you? It will give you an idea of how much difference they can make.

Icebreaker Examples

Icebreakers give everyone a chance to speak, which will increase the chances of them speaking up *again during* the meeting. They give people an insight into each other. They help build relationships. All of this leads to building trust.

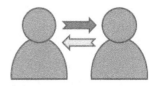

Here some good ones from Collaboration Superpowers: https://www.collaborationsuperpowers.com/44-icebreakers-for-virtual-teams/.

1. What was a favorite moment of [insert any time frame]?
2. What was your first job?
3. What is your favorite food? Drink?
4. Where is your favorite place to go on vacation?
5. What is your favorite smell?
6. Do you have any pets?
7. What is your favorite color?
8. Show your home on google maps and describe your environment: do you live near the city center? A park? A climbing gym? (courtesy of Morgan Legge)
9. What is your favorite movie?
10. Do you have a favorite music group, era, or album?

11. When I dance, I look like _____.

12. Share a favorite memory that includes food (courtesy of Sarah Baca)

13. What is the story of your name? (courtesy of Dr. Clue)

14. Take a picture from your window and have people guess where you are.

15. Show any picture from your life and tell the story behind it.

Another site is https://blog.pigeonholelive.com/20-company-ice-breakers-pigeonhole-live. If you want more, just search online for "online meeting icebreakers."

How to Refine Your Agenda for Your Specific Type of Meeting

> **Driving Principle: 6. Wasting Time**

It almost goes without saying that all meanings are not the same. Different types of meetings require different agendas that suit the needs of the meeting. If you have not tuned your agenda to the specific type of meeting you're having, then some people may see parts of the meeting as a waste of time.

Task Focused vs. Social Meetings

Task-focused meetings are meetings where the people are there to get something done, like team meetings, project meetings, and board meetings. People are there to make decisions, plans, address specific issues, and in general, get something done. They are not there to socialize. Here are some tips to make task meetings work:

- Stick to the agenda.
- Focus on the deliverables.
- Have check-in/ice-breaker time at the beginning but keep it to a minimum. Keep people on task. Don't let people run on and on about what happened this past weekend.
- Recommend to the attendees that they dress as though they were going to meet in the office.

Working Meetings vs. Information Sharing Meetings

Working meetings focus on making decisions, plans, or addressing some specific issue. Everyone involved in these meetings plays an active role in making the decisions or plans or providing essential information or perspective. Engagement is less of a problem because everyone should have at least one key part in the meeting. It is vital that you do *not* invite people who do not have an active role but just need the information. They will get bored and tune out.

Information sharing meetings focus on distributing information to many people. These meetings include announcing new policy changes, a new health plan, and meetings similar to conferences where only one or two people are presenting. The rest of the people are just sitting there watching and have little opportunity to contribute. Because of this, you should spend more time making it entertaining and doing things so that people will remember what was covered (learning). (See the tips a little later in this section about learning.) Make the slides simple and have just a few of them. Make the meeting relatively short. (Fraidenburg, Michael., 2020, p. 461). If you just want to waste their time and yours, have nice long meetings and overload the attendees with information in an hour-long lecture.

Fine Tune for a Common but Overlooked Process in Most Meetings—Learning

Even though your meeting is not a formal training meeting, people are still learning. All meetings involve people exchanging information. People are learning something new. It may be something important they should retain for a long time. It may be only useful for a brief time, like where a project stands or sales this week. But learning is still involved. Here are some tips from my book, *Designing Effective e-Learning*:

Manage Expectations: Make the meeting purpose, deliverables, and agenda clear. Make it clear if participants will be expected to do anything with what they learn. This will help them remember what was covered better because adults learn best when they have a need to know, and this will give it to them.

WIIFM—What's In It For Me: Make it clear how the attendees will benefit. If you do this as part of the meeting purpose and deliverables, it is pretty straightforward. (Same reason as above.)

Framework: Give them some kind of a framework or structure so that they can how the information is organized, how the pieces hang together, how they are connected.

Detail vs. High Level: Some people want detail. Some don't. Forcing those who don't like detailed reports to sit through them will turn them off. Solution? Present the high-level information in the meeting and provide ways for those who want the detail to get it after the meeting.

Data-oriented people vs. people-oriented people: Some people are interested in facts, numbers, data. Others are more interested in people and how they feel. Where possible, try to include both data and feelings as you cover topics. Example: "200,000 people now have had Covid. Here is how one mother felt when …"

Preferred Communication Mode: While there is conflicting evidence about this, be aware of these different modes. Try to use more than one mode if for no other reason than to increase variety and interest.

- Visual-Text: Prefers to *see* the information in *text* form
- Visual-Graphic: Prefers to *see* pictures and diagrams
- Kinesthetic: Prefers to learn by *doing* things
- Auditory: Prefers to *hear* about things

Limit the Load: Presenting a lot of material overloads short-term memory, so it never gets too long-term memory.

Ask Wrap-up Questions: Don't ask a simple "obvious answer" question like, *"Does everyone feel like they can ___?"* Instead, ask where people think they might find or have difficulty, something like, *"What problems do you think you might have ___?"* These

> **Thought Experiment 4**
>
> Read this number: 639-741. Close your eyes and repeat it. You probably got all 6 digits. Now try this one: 267-476-3549-808. Close your eyes and repeat. How many did you remember? Most people don't even get 6. They saw more but remembered less! This is a small example of information overload. Limit what you present to the really important stuff.

questions will help get people engaged and help you see where you might need to make changes in your presentation. Be sure to put these questions in your meeting leader's version of the agenda.

Finally, remember:

★ You can't teach anyone anything; you can only help them learn.

★ Learning is *not* a spectator sport. To really learn and remember something, people need to engage and use the information or skill.

> **Guideline 10: Identify what attendees are to learn. Present the information orally, in text form, and with graphics or images if possible. Give them time to practice using it.**

Regular vs. One-Time Meetings

Regular weekly or monthly meetings work better if you have a standard format for them. This way, people know what to expect and understand what their part is.

One-time meetings addressing specific issues call for you to spend more time getting truly clear about the deliverables. Don't set one up just to talk about some issues. Do your best to nail down precisely what you want to get out of the meeting regarding decisions, plans, and next steps.

Short vs. Long Meetings

> ## Driving Principle: 7. Distractions

Watch out for long meetings. Online, people are restricted to sitting in one place, staring at a screen. I have seen online conferences run all day long with a one-hour lunch break. Eight hours sitting on your fanny staring at a computer screen is too long—even with a lunch break and two short breaks.

- Any session without breaks that lasts longer than 30 minutes puts a heavy load on participant memory. The job of moving ideas presented into action becomes more difficult. It is just plain hard to remember all that stuff!
- Do all you can to shorten the meeting and still end up with the deliverables.
- Try not to let any one person talk for more than 10 minutes without others talking. Face-to-face you can get away with someone lecturing for longer, but online, people's attention will wander quickly.
- For long conferences, consider two half-day conferences, a week apart. People would have a week to assimilate and apply what they learned during the week. They might come back to the second session with good questions for the teacher or breakout room leader. The second session could build on what people learned and practiced.
- For long meetings, take a break every hour for at least 5 minutes.

New Faces vs. Familiar Faces

> ## Driving Principle: 2. Relationships

When the people in the meeting have a prior personal relationship, it's much less important to spend time getting to know each other. If you have any new faces around the table, you need to spend more time getting these people acquainted and creating new relationships so that the new people will trust each other.

Even when everyone around the table is a familiar face, don't shortchange their relationships. With the minimal contact that we have now in virtual meetings, there's a fair chance that the relationships will get weaker than if meeting in-person. Don't let that happen. Make at least some small amount of time for people to share successes in the meeting.

Ideas for Virtual Socials, Celebrations, and Parties

Some meetings are just for fun and to get to know each other better. These meetings are best suited to 20 people or less. Here are some things you can do in addition to the ice breakers above.

- Have a theme. Have people create some kind of room decorations and wear a costume.
- Before the meeting, have attendees set up their own food and drink so you can "break bread" online. If you are doing a theme, suggest people have that kind of food. Even have something as simple as your favorite seasonal snack
- Do a quick check-in. Be sure to give a time limit.
- Share a short video.
- Share photos.
- Have a virtual awards ceremony. Display and share the certificate on your computer during the meeting. Send it out after the meeting
- Have a talent show.
- Dance.
- Host a cocktail hour, wine tasting, or beer tasting.
- Host an ugly sweater show. Be careful that Aunt Martha, who gave you the sweater, doesn't watch.
- Create breakout rooms with assorted topics by naming the rooms. Send a list before the meeting. Open the rooms for 20 minutes and randomly assign people. They can leave when they want. Back in the main room, the host can put them in any room they want.

- Take a virtual field trip. The presenter prepares slides or videos in advance as though they were making a field trip and then shares them. Stop for questions as you go.
- Play some virtual games—here is one website: https://www.realsimple.com/work-life/entertainment/virtual-games.
- Have door prizes for the best costume. You can set up a digital door prize through most companies, including Amazon, and send them almost immediately. Have your tech support ready to send it, or have it cued up on your computer and just switch over to it and send with the winner's email.
- Tell the story behind your Christmas decoration.
- Recipes swaps.

Here is a link for online games. Also, search online for "virtual celebration ideas." https://teambuilding.com/blog/virtual-team-building-activities

And here is one more idea to get you thinking outside the box. The 2020 Peachtree Road Race here in Atlanta was run virtually! Each person ran their *own* 10K race. Apparently, they used some kind of app to track the runner's GPS coordinates and times. It's a very innovative way to hold a race that we thought *had* to be done in-person.

? Pause for a moment and do a quick self-check. How many of these ideas do you think would help you? It will give you an idea of how much difference they can make.

> **Guideline 11: Tune your agenda to the specific type of meeting you're having.**

Don't Be Too Proud

As you draft your agenda, it will, in some ways, dictate the different functions to be performed and who will do them. The bigger, the more complex the meeting, the more you will need people to support you, the meeting leader — people such as a greeter, minutes taker, timekeeper, technical support, and the different presenters in the meeting. Remember your job is to get the deliverables while engaging people and building relationships. It will be hard for you to do this if your attention is spread over many things.

Driving Principles: 1. Engagement, 2. Relationships

Technical Support Person

A meeting leader's role is to lead discussions, guide and manage a group event to ensure that the group's objectives are met effectively, and help participants stay involved. In addition to doing these, several technical things also need to be done. In small meetings, the leader can do these. But in larger meetings, attending to the technical details while at the same time conducting the meeting can be challenging. In these cases, it is a good idea to have a tech support person attend to technical details like these during the meeting:

- Start the meeting on a device.
- Admit people in from the waiting room if you are using one.
- Monitor the waiting room and be sure no one gets stuck there.
- Monitor participants in gallery view, looking for people who have distracting things going on.
  - Mute noisy people (crunching potato chips, a yelling child, a barking dog, etc.).
  - If a ceiling fan is spinning or something is going on in the background, contact them and see if they can make adjustments. Even if they can't for this meeting, maybe they will for the next one.
  - Send text messages if someone can improve their lighting or camera angle.
- Text or call people who were invited but have not shown up.
- Mute everyone or help them unmute themselves.
- Create breakout rooms, assign people to breakout rooms, and start the breakout room session.
- Take screenshots.
- Send messages to the breakout rooms.
- Assist participants who may need help with audio or video or something else via Zoom chat, phone chat, or a phone call.

- Monitor chat and alert the meeting host to any issues such as people not being able to hear. Respond as needed.
- Possibly start/present/share music and videos.

Hack 2: If the host is having trouble, the tech support person can request remote control of the host's computer and help. To do this, there may be options that need to be set before the meeting starts.

Meeting Emotions Monitor

Just like with technology, it's difficult for that person to be aware of all that's going on with the individuals in the meeting. A meeting monitor would be someone whose job it is to watch for subtle reactions or behaviors, identify people who were not engaged or showing signs of enthusiasm, agreement, boredom, or disagreement. The monitor would somehow report these observations to the meeting leader.

Greeter

For larger meetings where the host is busy, you may want a greeter. This person may monitor your waiting room and admit people. They could also send that person a welcome chat message. In rare cases, they could call people who said they would attend but have not to see if they need any help. This might be a job for the Meeting Monitor.

Minutes Taker

This one is pretty self-explanatory. Even in small meetings, it is not easy to take minutes *and* lead the meeting. This person could also watch the time and remind the leader if a topic is taking too long.

 Best Practice 4: Don't try to do it all yourself. Have people help with the meeting. This will keep them engaged.

Send Out the Invitation

At some point, you will need to send participants the meeting invitation.

- Send it out 2-3 days before the meeting.
- Send it out again the day of the meeting as a reminder.
- Put it on your website.
- In the email:
  - Include the link to the meeting **directly inline** in the email. Sometimes links in attachments don't work as planned.
  - List the meeting deliverables (objectives) and purpose as appropriate.
  - Include the agenda in as easily readable form as possible. Inline in the email rather than an attachment is a good idea.
  - Remind people to be ready to take notes if needed.
  - If you are spanning time zones, always specify which time zone. Even better, show several zones: 5 pm EST (4 pm CST, 2 pm PST).
  - If you have handouts, specify if they should be just read or printed for the meeting.
  - If you plan to use features like Reactions or Raise Hand, include some brief instructions until people are familiar with them.
  - Finally, include contact information if they have any kind of technical trouble.
- Remember to have a separate pre-meeting to practice using any new features or technology.

❓ Common Problems and How to Solve Them

Common Problem 8: The meeting is too long: Include stretch breaks for any meeting over an hour. Remember, in face-to-face meetings, people tend to move around as needed, and they have easy access to refreshments.

- If your meeting looks like it will need more than two hours, con-sider splitting it over several days or at least morning and after-noon sessions.

- Some writers recommend that you have people review documents before the meeting to save time during the meeting. In my experi-ence, this does not always work, especially if they are long. Some people will read them; some won't. You can try it and see how well it works with your participants.

Common Problem 9: Unprepared participants: Sometimes, attendees are not prepared for the meeting. They do not have or have not read what they need to have read. Send these out in plenty of time, and then send at least one or two reminders about how important they are to read.

Guideline 12: **Limit the number of pre-meeting documents to one or two. Make them short. Make that clear in the email.**

Common Problem 10: Not enough time for essential topics: Because technical problems are more likely, people frequently join the meet-ing late. Given that is the case, schedule time at the beginning of the meeting to cover a few less important things like welcome, introduc-tions, check-in, etc. After that, be sure to cover the more critical topics first because people get tired and distracted.

Common Problem 11: People looking bored: Build interactivity and engagement ideas into your agenda as much as possible. Have differ-ent people present, show slides, graphics, and videos. Use things like polls and breakout rooms where people are more engaged compared to sitting there listening.

Common Problem 12: Are people not participating partly because they do not know each other? Build in time for people to get ac-quainted.

Common Problem 13: Questions/Directions: When people have questions like, "Where are we?" set up a way for them to contact a designated person in the group and ask the question. For example, they could call, chat with, or text the tech support person. Make this known at the beginning of the meeting and put it as a footnote on the agenda.

Common Problem 14: Information Overload: If you are delivering lots of new information as in a training session or workshop, be sure to include time to practice. Remember, the common ingredient in all meetings—people. The constraint they all bring is their capacity to remember what was covered. Without practice, it is *unlikely* they will use what they learn.

Step 5: Get Proficient with the Online Meeting App Features

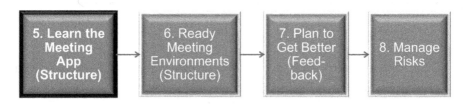

The technology you use is driven by the meeting purpose, deliverables, who is attending, the information presented, and what you will be doing. It is also driven by what is available to you and the other participants.

> **Driving Principles:** 1. Engagement, 6. Wasting Time, 7. Distractions

If you not proficient in the meeting app features you use, you will waste people's time and distract them from the meeting's purpose.

Select the Online Meeting App

If you are reading this book, you probably have already done this. Select and familiarize yourself with the features you will use in your meetings, such as showing a document or a video, playing music, chat, polls, breakout rooms, whiteboard, and more. Look over the settings. Be aware that some apps like Zoom have settings in two places, and they are different. One is on your device that controls video, audio, screen sharing, chat, recording, etc. The other place is online in your account. It covers many more settings.

YouTube is an excellent place to learn about the settings for your app. But don't depend on that alone. Try it yourself.

Make sure your name is displayed correctly, especially if you are using someone else's meeting account. I can't count the number of times I have seen "My iPhone" or some nickname that I did not recognize and gave no clue who the person was.

Guideline 13: Get proficient with as many meeting app features as you can to increase engagement and decrease distractions

---

Security—Waiting Room or Passcode?

More and more meeting apps are requiring increased security. Two common ones are a Waiting Room or a Passcode (password). You can use both, but I don't recommend that. Here are a few things to consider:

Waiting Room

Use a waiting room if you need to have a private conversation with one or two people just before the meeting starts. For example, if you are ironing out something with a presenter or maybe the music person, you may want them to join early and talk with you for a few minutes before the meeting starts.

Waiting Rooms require more of your attention. It is a good idea to have a tech support person admitting people if you have a meeting with five or more people.

Passcode

If you use a passcode, keep it simple. I recommend you use either all lower-case letters` or all numbers.

Keep it under seven letters or numbers.

Passcode takes less of your attention until someone loses it.

Dial-in people may have a problem if you use letters.

Both waiting rooms and passcodes require you to do something, usually in one or more settings, before the meeting starts. If you use a passcode, be sure it is included when you send out the meeting link.

Anyone who has a link to a public meeting can join. Links to public meetings may be traded in Facebook Groups and other chats. They are frequently easily discoverable on Twitter and public event pages. If your meeting is public, consider seriously using the waiting room.

Prepare to Use Breakout Rooms

Breakout rooms are an excellent way to get people engaged.

Setup Before the Meeting

If you plan to use breakout rooms, you may need to turn on some settings either on your computer or in your meeting app account online. Some apps provide the ability to pre-assign people to breakout rooms. Google can show you how to do this or check YouTube.

If you use breakout rooms, figure out the best way to get feedback from the breakout group back to everyone. Will they show a document? Will the report orally while you put responses on a whiteboard?

If the rooms are to address specific topics or answer some questions, you may need to have these sent to the attendees before the meeting.

Use During the Meeting

When you start the meeting, you need to create the rooms, assign people, set a breakout room timer, and open the breakrooms. When you open the rooms, the people can only see the other people in their room. You may want to send messages to the rooms, and you may want to join one or more. It can get a bit confusing. Here is a wonderful place to have a tech support person working with you.

While breakout rooms may sound easy, they can be tricky. Practice assigning people to a specific breakout room. Practice moving people from one room to another. Practice setting how long it will run. Practice sending messages to the breakout rooms. Practice doing it more than once in a meeting.

Prepare to Take Screen Shots

If you are not recording your meeting and even if you are, consider using a screen capture tool to grab all or some of the screen in screenshots for later use. These tools can be set up to store what they capture to a file or directly into a document with just a hotkey press. If you are using online whiteboards or the like, this can help send out follow-up messages. (Fraidenburg, Michael., 2020, p. 22)

Prepare to Conduct a Poll

If you have decided to use a poll, try it out before the meeting. Each meeting app does this differently. Search online for how to do this. Be sure to practice displaying the results to the participants after the poll is closed. Also, figure out how to save the results of the poll if needed.

Prepare to Use Chat

Chat allows you to send text messages to everyone or just one person. If you've never used it, you should practice a couple of times.

Hack 3: Zoom allows you to save the chat either manually or automatically. Other apps may allow this too, but you'll have to check out how for any specific app.

Hack 4: You can also use chat to send files to the whole group or individuals.

Prepare to Use an Online Whiteboard

When you have participants work on something and want everyone to contribute ideas, it is useful to record the ideas visually. You can use the app's built-in whiteboard, or you can share another document.

The whiteboard can be useful, but it has limitations. Sometimes a more practical choice is to use a Word or PowerPoint document and show it on your computer through the meeting app. (This is called "sharing" something. Sharing does not mean you send it via email.) Then you can easily edit the document after the meeting is over and send it out. Here is a brief comparison of the more apparent features to help you make your decision.

App Whiteboard	Document
Participants can enter info themselves, although this may take some learning on their part. This approach is useful if you plan to do this frequently, and the participants can get used to the whiteboard controls.	Only the person sharing the document can enter and change information because it resides only on their computer. (See exception below.)
Changes are not easy to make during the meeting.	Changes are relatively easy.
If you want to distribute it after the meeting, you *must* save it *during* the meeting because after you end the meeting is no longer available.	You would save the document as you usually would.
Saved whiteboards are pictures (JPGs or PNGs) and can only be edited with an application that can edit photos.	Changes are easy to make, such as reformatting, rewording, rearranging, etc.
No advance setup is possible.	You can set up your document in advance with titles, sections, graphics, etc.

Hack 5: If you want two people to simultaneously edit the same document, have an attendee request remote control of the presenter's screen. Then both the speaker and that attendee can write on the document.

Hack 6: If you want to show two documents simultaneously, share your *desktop* instead of a document. Open both documents and arrange them so that both can be seen on your desktop. Then participants can see them both at the same time.

Hack 7: Using the above Hack, you can see the speaker at the same time as showing a document. Examples would be 1) someone talking about the bible who wanted to be seen and have the bible verses show, or 2) someone singing live and wanting the words shown below. In Zoom, click Stop Video to turn off your camera, start the computer camera app (not the Zoom one), and start the document you want to show. Then share your desktop. Since this is a little tricky, you may need tech support to do this.

Prepare to Record Your Meeting

If you decide to record a meeting, know that every minute takes about 10mb. So, for a 1-hour meeting, you are looking at around 600MB, which is way too much to send via email. Some apps like Zoom provide cloud recording. Then you can give people links to the meeting they missed. You can find out more details on YouTube. For Zoom, the coverage in James Bernstein's book, *Zoom Made Easy: Establishing Lasting Connections*, Kindle Edition is pretty good.

Prepare to Play Music or Videos

Sometimes you will want to play some music or show a video. These can come directly from your computer (recommended) or from something like YouTube. While I have successfully shown YouTube videos, it does add another layer of complexity. The video has to 1) come from YouTube to the presenting computer, 2) then the meeting app has to capture it as it is playing and send it *back* to the internet;

and finally, 3) the meeting app has to send it from the internet to the people in the meeting.

If you plan to do this, open the music or video on your computer before the meeting and pause it. This will avoid you spending valuable meeting time hunting around for it during the meeting. And be sure to have them readily available in case the open music or video app closes by accident.

When you are done, close the video *before* you stop sharing. I have seen the video start playing again after the sharing window was closed. Because the meeting window covers most of the screen now, it makes the video very hard to find. It seriously confused things.

Important Note: If you are sharing in an environment with significant background noise, try muting yourself. In Zoom, this will turn off your microphone but not the sound from the video. Not sure about other apps.

Participants Sharing Documents, Music, Videos

If you want to have participants share something during the meeting, you will likely have to adjust some settings before the meeting. Check your meeting app to see what is available.

An alternative is to make a participant a co-host during the meeting (if your app allows this). Learn how to do this well before the meeting and practice with a friend.

In all cases, make sure the participant has a reliable high-speed internet connection.

Be Sure You Know How to Mute Everyone

People in their home environment may be unaware of babies crying, dogs barking, construction hammering, or car horns honking because they are familiar to that person.

Experience may be the best teacher, but ...

I have heard of one meeting where everyone was forced to listen to someone munching on chips for 20 long minutes.

In another meeting, one person had to blow their nose from time to time. He was sitting close to the camera so all you really saw was his face. When he blew his nose, people who were on speaker view suddenly saw a closeup of her instead of the current presenter.

Learn how to mute a given person or mute everyone and alert people when they start talking that they are still muted.

Other Settings for a Better Meeting

Where these settings are and what options you will have depends on the meeting app you are using.

Sound notification when someone joins or leaves: I recommend you set this so that only the host and co-hosts will hear the sound; otherwise when people leave or join, it could be distracting.

Co-host: It is probably a good idea to turn this one on for a couple of reasons. First, if you have a tech support person, you will likely be making them a co-host. Second, if you limit sharing to the host only, then if you want someone to share something from their device, you will need to make them a co-host.

There are many more settings. At some point, you probably should review them all so that you know what is available.

? Common Problems and How to Solve Them

Common Problem 15: Low video or audio quality: Have your device as close to your router as possible. Close all non-essential apps on your device, especially other browser windows. Ask other people using the same router or internet connection to limit their use during your meeting. For example, if you are broadcasting from your home office, ask the teenagers to hold off playing online games or streaming video while your meeting is in progress.

Common Problem 16: Computer or internet connection failure: Have a backup plan for serious computer problems or failure, lost files, broken internet connections, etc. One straightforward way is to have a backup host/presenter. Give them all the files needed and have them on standby.

Common Problem 17: Uninvited guests: If you have any reason to think you might have uninvited guests or troublemakers, check out the security measures your meeting app provides. Try them out so you can use them if needed, like removing an unwanted guest from the meeting.

Common Problem 18: Participants have technical troubles: Remind people of the meeting ahead of time. If you are having new people attend, consider running a trial meeting an hour earlier so they can resolve any problems. Have a tech support person available to attend to these issues.

Make sure that people have and will use appropriate technology. Check with new people in a test meeting to be sure they can connect, hear, and see you, and you can hear and see them.

Common Problem 19: General technical difficulties: Have someone either in the meeting or on standby who is good with technology and familiar with your meeting app to help if needed.

Common Problem 20: Fumbling with unfamiliar meeting app features: If you are considering using features like whiteboards, breakout rooms, polls, or sharing the screen that you have not used before, be sure to try these out in a practice session well before your meeting. They aren't always as easy as they appear on YouTube.

Common Problem 21: Singing along with the music: Sometimes, people want to sing along with a song that is playing, especially if the lyrics are being shown. There is a significant time lag involved because of all that has to happen: voices are captured by microphones, transmitted to the internet, then back down to someone's computer, and finally played on speakers. Participant singing is usually out of sync with the music. It can be very distracting. It is a good idea for the host to mute everyone until the music is over. Remember, you are *not* meeting in person, so the energy is different. Listening to music alone is quite different from being in a room full of people singing along.

Common Problem 22: Pictures freeze: During the meeting or people report that *your* picture is frozen. The most common reason is internet speed. You should have a minimum of 5Mbps upload and 30 download. You can easily check your internet speed by going to www.speedtest.net.

Tech Wrap-up

Remember that online meetings have many more "moving parts." Whatever you decide to use, you need to look at it from two perspectives.

- Your perspective: What is best for the meeting? Can I use it smoothly, maybe with the help of a tech support person?
- Participant perspective: Will they be able to understand how to use this stuff? Will they know what to click to write on the whiteboard? Will going in and out of a breakout room confuse them? Etc.

Hack 8: It's not always easy to find someone to test app features with, and you don't get a complete view of what they see if they're not in your location and you can see what they see. One way around that and to practice is to open a meeting on one device and then log into the meeting with a couple of your own devices. Maybe you have one computer and your spouse has another one. You can sign in to Zoom as the same person on both computers and create a meeting with those two computers. You could also use a cell phone or a tablet.

And one story about an experienced meeting host who ran slap into a wall.

Experience may be the best teacher, but it is *expensive!*

Recently I was the tech support person for someone who had run a meeting with the same group of people half a dozen times. It was Christmas and he had sent out a nice holiday invitation to the meeting in a PDF attached to an email. The invitation had the link to the meeting which included a password. It turned out that for some strange reason when people clicked the link in the PDF, they we're asked for the password which was not printed for safety reasons. This had never happened before when we had included the link *directly* in the email. As a result, many people had difficulty getting in and a few never got into the Christmas meeting.

 Best Practice 5: Try new things out *before* the real meeting in a practice one with a friend.

Best Practice 6: Test everything frequently. Technology changes moment by moment. The day before the meeting, test. Fifteen minutes before the meeting, test.

Step 6: Ready the Meeting Environments

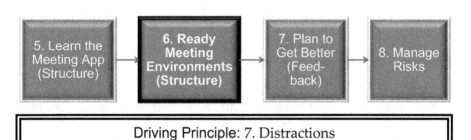

Your environment is the place you will be "broadcasting" from. You will want to configure it so that it supports you in the meeting. Give some attention to lighting, camera angle, distractions, comfortable seating, comfortable air temperature, and refreshments for long meetings.

It is essential to properly prepare for a
Zoom meeting

Warning 10: **Online meetings are mostly held in environments that were *not* designed for meetings —your home office. Some "remodeling" may be needed at your home *and* at the attendee's homes.**

(Credit to an unknown author)

First, Some Important Hardware Tips

Use the Best Device

I highly recommend you join meetings using a computer if possible. If you are leading many meetings or presenting regularly, get serious, and get a good computer.

- Devices like phones and tablets will limit seeing all the people who attend.
- From time to time, the presenter may be showing documents or a whiteboard in the meeting. They are much easier to read on a computer than on a smartphone or a tablet.
- Good camera angles may be difficult to attain. Resting a phone or tablet on your desk can result in viewers looking up your nose, getting a view of just your head, and missing a lot of your body language.

Best Practice 7: For important meetings, have more than one device ready in case of problems, maybe even a backup location and meeting leader.

In our experience, problems happen. For many reasons, your primary device may not work correctly (poor connection, camera, microphone, or speaker do not work, ...). So, get your computer ready *and* have your phone or tablet ready too.

Close applications other than your meeting app during the session so your device can devote as much of its resources as possible to your meeting. Limiting applications will make your meeting app run smoother.

Have a Good Internet Connection

MOST IMPORTANT: Check your WiFi signal strength . Be close to your router. You should have as many bars as possible on the WiFi signal icon.

Hack 9: You can also connect directly to your internet router using an Ethernet cable. This will improve the quality of your connection. Remember to turn off WiFi on your computer once you are plugged in and connected with the Ethernet cable. If you have a computer that does not have an Ethernet cable socket, you can get an Ethernet to USB adaptor from Amazon starting at about $12.

Turn off any TV that may be using the internet. Cable shows do not. Netflix does.

Ask others who share your internet connection to minimize internet use while you are in the meeting (i.e., turn off Netflix, stop playing online games).

You should have a minimum of 5Mbps upload and 30Mbps download. You can quickly check your internet speed by going to www.speedtest.net.

Guideline 14: All this boils down to: Use a computer with an adequate internet connection.

Can You Hear?

Check to be sure your device speakers are working. If you have used them in the last few days, then skip to the next item. If not, try playing some music on your computer. If you don't have any, go to www.youtube.com and click on something. Click the play arrow, and you should hear some music.

- If not, you may need to increase the volume. How you do that depends on your computer and keyboard. On your keyboard, look for a key that has a speaker icon like this on it 🔊. If it is on top or above another key along the top of your keyboard like F6, F7, … F12, you may need to press and hold the FN key in the lower row of your keyboard while taping the speaker key with your other hand.
- If you are using external speakers, make sure they are plugged in, have the proper power, and their own volume knob is set correctly.
- If that does not work, get help before the meeting.

Can They Hear You?

Probably the easiest way to check your microphone is to access your meeting app settings on your computer. Zoom has a way to check your microphone. I am guessing the rest do.

If you are ever likely to want to share your screen or audio files or video with audio, you may need to unplug any headphones or external microphone so that the internal computer microphone works. How to unplug them varies with different computers. It's a good idea to try this in a private meeting with a friend.

How to Get The Rest of Your Environment Ready

Ready Yourself

Something people forget is how they dress. They are at home. Casual is fine. But you are in meeting with other people where face-to-face you would be dressed differently. (True story: I forgot this tip one morning and attended a men's group meeting in my pajamas. I got some serious ribbing!) The more formal the meeting, the better you should dress, especially if you lead the meeting or present. "Dress for success." Solid colors are better as it is easier for the camera to keep them in focus. Look at yourself on screen 15 minutes before the meeting. Ask yourself, "Would I pay attention to that person?" (Try not to laugh too hard ☺.)

Prepare for Your Presenter's Notes

If you will be presenting, figure out now where and how you will view your notes. In-person you would have them printed on the podium. When online, you have choices. Don't make the wrong one—printed lying on your laptop keyboard. Here are some options I have seen used:

- Printed lying on the desk *beside* the computer. This is a not-so-good choice because the audience can see you break eye contact. Plus, it may not work so well if you are standing.
- Use a second screen with your computer or have a second computer. (Fraidenburg, Michael., 2020, p. 17)
- If you are *not* presenting visuals like a PowerPoint slide deck, you can overlay the meeting app with your speaker's notes on the computer screen. Then they are right in front of you. And no, you can't see your audience. That can be a reason *not* to do this. Try it and see if it works for you.
- Use a podium. OK, you don't want to spend the money, nor do you have a place to store it. Try using an inexpensive music stand. Amazon has them for less than $15.

Ready Your Room

> **Guideline 15:** **Configure your "meeting room" to be comfortable, look professional, and be free from distractions.**

Pick a room where there are few distractions or interruptions if possible. Turn off overhead lights or fans if they show in your camera. They can be very distracting.

Close the door. Just search online for "meeting mistakes," and you will laugh at the number of times a naked spouse walked past the door which was in the camera. If you can't close the door, try to arrange the camera to avoid the door.

Aim the camera at a quiet professional wall. Simple walls are the best. Bookcases work fine as long as there is nothing too distracting in them. Do not aim the camera at a window where there may be activity such as traffic or birds. People will watch these instead of focusing on the meeting. Consider using a virtual background if you don't have a good background. Check your meeting app to see how to do this. Remember, your goal is to draw attention to you, not your background.

Hack 10: If you will be presenting and the meeting is more like a conference or training session, then see if you can place the computer so you can stand while talking. Presenters who speak while standing are more powerful than when sitting. You can put the laptop on a box or shelf or get an easily adjustable laptop stand. Some even have a place for a mouse.

Talk to other people in the building like relatives or co-workers and let them know you will be in a meeting. Get someone else to herd the children.

Adjust the room temperature to suit your needs. With the door closed, it sometimes can get a bit warm. Maybe have an electric fan or turn on your A/C circulating fan. If you turn on a ceiling fan, make sure it does not show in your camera.

Get Some Refreshments for Long Meetings

Drinking is usually accepted in shorter working meetings. Longer interactive ones where others can see you, clear it with the host or presenter first. Make sure eating is okay before you chow down.

Short meeting? Skip this. Long ones, plan ahead. In long face-to-face meetings, the host usually provides refreshments such as water, juice, coffee, soda, and snacks within easy access of the meeting, so if you need some, you don't have to miss any of the meeting. But at home, we have all this stuff in the kitchen, which means you have to leave the meeting room to get them. And then, on the way, you will be attacked by the kids, husband, or a well-meaning friend.

Head this off! Have a cooler nearby with drinks. Have some snacks within easy reach. And hey, if you're in lots of meetings, maybe you want to get a mini-fridge for your computer room.

Have a Good Chair

If your meetings will be long or you have many of them, get a comfortable chair that has adjustments. Sitting in one position for extended periods can wear on you, and you might not even notice it. A chair with arms is preferable. One that rolls around is good. If you are uncomfortable, this can be a significant distraction during a meeting.

How to Like the Way You Look in an Online Meeting

Most people will be using a computer or device camera when they are in an online meeting. Here are a couple of ways to test your camera and see how you look in your surroundings and lighting:

- Turn on your device camera (look for the camera app on your computer) or
- Look for a setting in your meeting app or
- Just start a meeting with just yourself.

Two important things to consider are lighting and camera angle.

Have the Right Lighting

The cameras work better when the light comes from in *front* of you, and there is *minimal* light *behind* you. If there is a lot of light behind you, either move or try to block some of the light by turning it off or closing blinds or curtains. *"The main rule to remember is that the background should never have more light than the foreground."* (Foley, 2020).

Figure 9: Too much backlight

Hack 11: Before you go too far with making lighting changes, consider getting some software to enhance your camera. These apps give you the ability to change the color, brightness, and contrast. Here are a few I have found that are either free or exceptionally low cost. I have only tried iGlasses on a Mac, and it works well. I have not tried any of the ones for Windows. There are many others. Search for "iGlasses alternatives" or "iGlasses for Windows."

MyCam	Windows	Free or $9.99	https://www.e2esoft.com/mycam/
YouCam 9	Windows	Free or $34.99	https://www.cyberlink.com/products/youcam/features_en_US.html
Webcamoid	Windows	Free	https://webcamoid.github.io/
iGlasses	iMac	$19.95	https://www.ecamm.com/mac/iglasses/

Additional lighting can help if you are concerned about wrinkles or brown spots on your face. Consider getting a camera ring light used for YouTube video/photography.

Figure 10: Ring light

Ring lights can vary the brightness as well as the warmth of the light they project onto your video. Just search for "ring light" on Amazon. Get one that *plugs into the wall or your computer, NOT* a battery-powered one. The battery ones are not bright enough, and they may not have enough power to last through long meetings. You can purchase a good ring light for $50-$70.

My Wife's Advice on Getting a Flattering Picture

You can minimize lines in your neck and a double chin significantly by raising your computer slightly, so the camera is just *above* your eye level. A ring light placed behind your computer will minimize wrinkles, brown spots, and other skin problems on your face. This picture was taken with a ring light on a medium setting with a bluer tone. She played with the ring light for a couple of minutes to find the most flattering light for her.

Another small thing you can do is to check the meeting app settings. In Zoom, you have the Touch up my appearance setting.

My Video: ☐ Enable HD

☐ Mirror my video

☑ Touch up my appearance

Use a Sane Camera Angle

Besides the lighting, it is good to have the camera at eye level. If you are looking down or up at the camera/screen, your face will be somewhat distorted. If you use a laptop, put some books under it so that the camera is right at eye level. If you are using a phone or tablet, see if you can put it on a box or something.

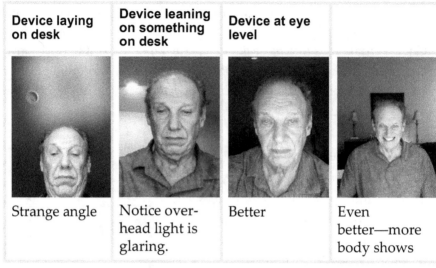

Device laying on desk	Device leaning on something on desk	Device at eye level	
Strange angle	Notice over-head light is glaring.	Better	Even better—more body shows

Figure 11: Camera Angles

"the camera lens always needs to be at eye level. Always! If it isn't, you risk having your viewers staring at your chin instead of your face; or getting dizzy from watching your ceiling fan spin around; or becoming distracted by whatever else is going on in the background. By getting the angle and framing right, people can see you in a way that mimics you sitting across the table from them. This is the goal, because it makes it easier for them to look at your face, connect, and engage." (Foley, 2020)

Hack 12: IMPORTANT: Because body language is so important in communication, it is better to sit back a little from the camera, so most of the top half of your body is in the frame. This is how we usually see people in a meeting. Check out newscasters on TV. You see more than just their face.

Make sure your whole face is in view of the camera. If you and someone else are attending the same meeting together on one computer, make sure *both* of you are visible.

Check *behind* you. Remove distracting objects. Dim lights. Block daylight streaming in through a window.

Check *above* you. Turn off ceiling fans. Dim overhead lights that show in the camera.

Other Tips

You also might want to check these out:

- *How To Look Good on Video Calls*
  https://www.youtube.com/watch?v=ACNGhPKnmok
- *How to look sharp for webcam meetings*
  https://www.digitaltrends.com/mobile/how-to-look-sharp-for-webcam-meetings/

? Pause for a moment and do a quick self-check. How many of these ideas do you think would help you? It will give you an idea of how much difference they can make.

Help Your Participants Upgrade *Their* Environments

Driving Principles: 1. Engagement, 7. Distractions

By helping your participants ready their environments, they will stay more engaged because they won't be distracted. Plus, others in the meeting won't be distracted either.

If you have new people in your meeting, consider giving them a hand with their environment/location. Make these suggestions in an email separate from the invitation.

Technology

- Use a computer rather than a tablet or phone.
- Double check their internet connection and speed.
- Have a backup device ready if at all possible.
- Check their computer speakers and microphone.
- Make sure their name is displayed correctly, especially if you are using someone else's meeting account.
- Have the camera at eye level. Do not aim at the ceiling where there is a running overhead fan.

- Check the lighting to avoid being back-lit.
- Join the meeting a few minutes early in case of any tech problems.

Ready the Room

- Tell others in the house you will be in a meeting.
- Close the door.
- Get a comfortable chair.
- Adjust the temperature.
- Have some refreshments for long meetings.
- Print any handouts.

IMPORTANT: Have good lighting and a good camera angle. Explain to people that it is important to communicate as much body language as possible because it is extremely limited in online meetings. Since something like 55% of communication is done through body language, this dramatically limits building strong relationships. This will also help the people who are presenting and hosting the meeting do a better job because they will be better able to "read" their audience.

 Best Practice 8: The bottom line for environments is to spend some time and energy adapting them for online meetings to minimize distractions and maximize engagement.

Step 7: Plan to Get Better

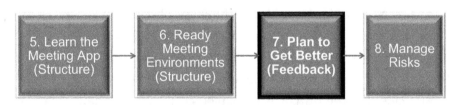

Without feedback, you are doomed to make the same mistakes again and not even know it! If you are serious about conducting effective meetings, you must get feedback. Take time now to plan the questions you will use to get feedback on your meeting.

| Driving Principle: 8. Follow-up |

Feedback Behind Your Back

In volunteer environments, people just don't show up again if they didn't get what they wanted. That's a tough way to find out your meeting had problems. In business, people are usually required to attend. Negative feedback might be that people grumble behind your back, don't implement decisions or next steps, don't apply what they learned, etc. Again, a hard way to get feedback.

Nearly Useless Feedback

Let's look at some common but nearly useless feedback questions. Below are a few I found on the internet that rated things on a 5-point scale. The problem with this kind of feedback is that if you get low ratings, you have little if any idea about what to correct.

Question	Problem
How would you rate this meeting?	Rate what? The whole meeting? What if some parts were good and others not so good? If someone rates the meeting low, why? With this question, you have no idea what to fix.
Was this a successful meeting?	If so, why? If not, why not? What would make it more successful? What are your criteria for success? It could be a lot of things.
Did we come to the meeting prepared, and did we follow the agenda?	How does one answer if we came prepared but did not follow the agenda? Avoid compound questions.

Question	Problem
Was the team engaged (was everyone heard)?	Most people are not aware of how much they talk or of people who don't talk. They do remember people who monopolized the meeting.
Were we open and honest?	How would someone really know?
Did we solve a real issue forever?	Forever? Really? How do you rate this on a 5-point scale?

And even if you have better questions, a 5-point scale does not really tell you something you can use. They are closed questions. If something was wrong, but you did not have a question on that specific topic, then you will have no idea there is a problem. Instead, use open questions that allow people to tell you something useful.

Simple but Useful Feedback

This feedback is simple and easy to do and is certainly light years away from none at all. It uses open-ended questions, which are usually more helpful than rating scales. These are short, so people are more likely to get them back to you.

You just ask, "What worked?" "What didn't?" in two areas.

Feedback on the **Deliverables:**
- What helped us create the deliverables for this meeting?
- What got in the way? What could we have done better?

Feedback on the **Experience** (how people *felt* about the meeting, how it was run):
- What made this a great experience?
- What things didn't work so well? What could we change to make it better?

I recommend you ask separate questions about the goals or deliverables and the experience. You can imagine having a meeting where you got your deliverables, but it was a rough experience. You can also imagine the opposite, a great meeting experience but you didn't achieve the goals. By asking them separately, you help people focus on the two distinct aspects of a meeting.

Note: Most people will not be aware that something got in the way of building relationships. These processes are well hidden, and we take them for granted. So, if something did get in the way, most people will not give feedback about it. The best they're going to be able to do is say that something didn't feel good or right.

As part of your plan, consider introducing these questions as you close out the meeting. Explain how this will help. Then send them out and pray a lot!

> Guideline 16: **Draft your feedback questions to find out what worked and what didn't for your deliverables and for how participants experienced the meeting.**

Feedback for Regular Small-Group Meetings

Small groups frequently meet regularly, like monthly or weekly. In this case, it is a little less important to have written feedback because once you get rolling, you've ironed out the usual problems. What is more important is to get with people one-on-one periodically. Say, for example, you have a team with five members, and you meet weekly. Then meet with the team members one-on-one at least once a month and talk with each one about how they see the meetings are going. Ask the questions listed above and any others that seem relevant.

 Best Practice 9: Plan to get and give feedback so your meetings get better.

? Common Problems and How to Solve Them

Common Problem 23: Not anonymous—some people may not want to say something negative that needs to be said, so using email will identify who said what. Try using something like www.survey-monkey.com. When I last checked, it did support questions like the open ones above.

Common Problem 24: Few people send in feedback—Call a few on the phone and ask them if they sent in feedback. If not, why not?

Step 8: If Something Can Go Wrong, It Will! Be Prepared

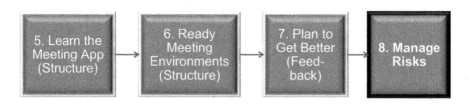

The bigger, the more important the meeting, the more you need to assess and manage your risks. If yours is an *informal* meeting, you can skip this step entirely.

Risk assessment and management are easy. I will not talk about any math here, just a simple way to think about risks. Don't let anyone make you think it is hard. It just takes a bit of time and focus. Let's start with getting a better handle on just what risk management is.

Simplified Risk Management

Here are six easy-to-understand properties of risks. Let's use the example of a car crash and limit ourselves to one item for each property while, in reality, there are many.

Property	Example
1. The **risk event**—something that might go wrong and have an impact.	Your car crashing into another
2. **Likelihood**—how likely (the probability) the event is to happen. The more likely, the more you need to prepare.	Very low
3. **Impact**—if the event occurs, what is the effect?	Could result in serious property damage and serious personal injury or death
4. **Risk Avoidance**—how can you reduce the chances of the event occurring at all?	Keep the car well maintained, especially tires & breaks, drive safely, drive vehicles with high crash-*avoidance* ratings (approaching vehicle indicators, crash imminent braking)
5. **Impact Reduction**—what can you do to reduce the impact of the event if it does occur?	Drive cars with high safety and crashworthiness ratings like crushable bumpers, side airbags, etc., wear your seat belt
6. **Contingency Plans**—what might you do afterward if the event happens?	Have a first-aid kit in the car, have your mobile phone available, have insurance

Figure 12: Risk Properties

For simplicity, start out using a simple scale of High, Medium/Moderate, Low for Likelihood.

The following pages show some examples of risk analysis for an online meeting. I recommend you do yours in a spreadsheet so you can sort or filter to find the more severe risks easily.

 Warning 11: **The following is *not* meant to be a complete list of risks and solutions. Each meeting situation is different. Get help identifying and managing *your* risks. In this case, two heads are better than one.**

Note: The tables that follow are broken into two parts because this book is not wide enough to have them side by side.

These tables show several risks combined, which may work fine. If they are distinctly different, separate them into different tables (or rows) like the one on People Risks.

Example Agenda Risks

Risk Event	Likelihood	Impact
Poorly designed meeting with no purpose/deliverables, too long, wrong time of day, too many or not enough people, low interactivity, too much information, lack of variety, no breaks	Low	Moderate to high

How to Reduce the Likelihood	How to Reduce Impact	Contingency Plans
Follow the guidelines in this book. Have someone else review your meeting plan.	Facilitate even more Consciously keep people involved	Get feedback so you can avoid recurrence.

Example Environment/Location Risks

Risk Event	Likelihood	Impact
Poor lighting or camera angle Background noise or visual distraction	Low	Low

How to Reduce the Likelihood	How to Reduce Impact	Contingency Plans
Check out what you look like by doing a test call. Warn husband and have him take care of the kids. Close and lock the door.	Warn people at the beginning of the meeting there may be a problem.	Apologize and don't let it happen again.

Example People Risks

Risk Event 1	Likelihood	Impact
Leader/speaker cannot make meeting Poor presenter (not spoken before, not prepared, poor talk subject or content, poor slides)	Moderate	Moderate

How to Reduce the Likelihood	How to Reduce Impact	Contingency Plans
Check with presenters the day before the meeting. Vet the presenters.	Be ready to step in and help presenter	Have back-up presenters ready.

Risk Event 2	Likelihood	Impact
Invitations not sent, lost, or incorrect	Low	Moderate

How to Reduce the Likelihood	How to Reduce Impact	Contingency Plans
Verify some people have received the invitation.	Have tech person call people who are not there at beginning	Have your tech person help people who cannot get on.

Example Technology Risks

Risk Event	Likelihood	Impact
Serious computer problems or failure Lost files that were to be displayed (documents, music, videos) Poor internet connection No internet connection Security—uninvited guests Participants cannot join or have other technical troubles	Low to medium	High

How to Reduce the Likelihood	How to Reduce Impact	Contingency Plans
Test everything before the meeting. Implement and test appropriate security measures available for your app. Set up something so new people can try getting on early and resolve their tech problems.	Have a tech person on standby.	Have a backup device with all the necessary files loaded and connections tested. Have a backup person with copies of everything.

 Best Practice 10: For important meetings, take the time to analyze the risks and prepare.

Critical Success Factors *Planning* a "Suck-free" Meeting

This chapter covered a lot of ground. One effective way to apply all this is to take it step by step when planning your next meeting. That will help you get a little bit better handle on what to do. Then for the meeting after that, try just using the checklist at the beginning of the chapter. When you have a gap or run across something you don't remember, just read that step.

Here are a few critical things you need to address in your plan to increase your success.

Factor	What You Need to Do
1. Attention to relationships	✓ Plan opportunities for people to create and build relationships.
2. Direction clarity	✓ Be very clear about the purpose and deliverables of your meeting.
3. Minimizing boredom	✓ Long online meetings are harder on people than in-person ones—design in variety. Keep people engaged.

Factor	What You Need to Do
4. Reducing Distractions	✓ Help attendees configure a low-distraction environment for themselves. Practice new app features so that it goes smoothly during the meeting.
5. Practice	✓ Get comfortable with all the tech you plan to use. Test, test, test. Practice until you are very familiar with it. Remember the story about the Christmas invitation that went awry. If you decide to do *anything* new, be sure to try it out before the big day.

Chapter 4

Treatment II: Run "Suck-free" Online Meetings

All your prep work is done. "Curtain going up." Adrenalin going up with it!

I'm guessing that if you're reading this, you have already run some face-to-face meetings. Running online meetings is very much the same except that you need to pay more conscious attention to keeping people engaged, building relationships, and sticking to the agenda. This chapter will help you do that.

Figure 13: Process of Running an Online Meeting

On the next page is an easy checklist to use as you prepare for and run an online meeting. Once you've read through this chapter, you'll be able to do most of your work with just the checklist. If you forget something, simply reread that section of this chapter.

Checklist for Running a "Suckfree" Meeting

Preparing

☐ Verify support staff is ready.

☐ Check your Internet connection and turn off other devices using the Internet.

☐ Get your computer ready by turning off unnecessary apps and opening documents you will use or share.

☐ Open the meeting portal 10-15 minutes early.

☐ Have your leader's version of the agenda printed.

During the Meeting

☐ Open by welcoming people and doing some kind of check-in.

☐ If this is a new group, agree on etiquette.

☐ Facilitate, don't dictate.

☐ Keep all participants engaged by asking your preplanned questions.

☐ Keep people from monopolizing the conversation.

☐ Watch for people being distracted and body language. Adjust accordingly.

☐ Stick to the agenda focusing on deliverables and bring closure to each topic as it is covered.

Presenting

☐ Mute everyone so no accidental sounds distract from the presenter.

☐ Speak from a standing position.

☐ Look directly at the camera, not at the screen.

☐ Move back from the camera so people can read more of your body language.

☐ Don't talk too long without asking questions to keep people involved.

☐ Ask for simple feedback like head nods.

☐ When you're done, make it clear that you're giving control back to the host.

Ending the Meeting

☐ Summarize accomplishments making it clear that you reached your goals/deliverables.

☐ Thank everyone.

☐ Remind them that you will be asking for feedback.

Step 1: Get Prepared—Avoid Tech Glitches

Driving Principle: 6. Wasting Time

Being prepared, starting early, makes for better delivery. Here are the essential things you should address:

✓ Verify that presenters, greeter, minutes taker, timekeeper, and tech support are ready.

✓ Ask others who share your internet connection to minimize internet use while you are in the meeting (i.e., turn off Netflix, stop playing online games).

✓ Turn off any TV that may be using the internet.

✓ Close any app/window on your computer that is not needed for the meeting.

✓ Check your Wi-Fi signal strength .

✓ Open any documents, videos, or music you are going to share. A good practice here is to have these documents on the computer desktop, so you can find them quickly if they accidentally get closed.

✓ Open the meeting portal early. Invite people to join the meeting early so they can iron out technical problems. If they have none, they can just spend time together and talk with each other.

✓ Until you are very experienced, print a copy of the leader's version of the agenda with all your questions you plan to ask and your reminders and tips.

Best Practice 11: Be prepared. Start the meeting early so that you have time to recover if there is a problem.

Step 2: Facilitate the Meeting

Driving Principles: All of them

What you do during an online meeting is similar to face-to-face meetings, but there are some crucial differences.

- Sticking to the agenda is a little more important because of the time constraints and the likelihood of distractions. Remember, it is more likely that some people will just sit and watch and not participate.
- Facilitating becomes even more critical to keep people engaged.
- And once more, if you are using any new technology or feature of the meeting app, be sure to have practiced using it.

Open the Meeting

Welcome new people. Have others check-in.

Make sure the purpose and deliverables are clear.

Announce planned breaks so people know what to expect and when they can get coffee.

Be sure to get agreement on etiquette like these points, especially if this is the first meeting with these people.

- Don't monopolize
- Participate
- Parking lot
- Distractions
- Interrupting

If this is to be a long meeting or has several sessions like a conference, suggest people take notes.

 **Best Practice 12: Open the meeting by making it clear
what the goals are and building relationships by having
others check-in.**

Tips for Facilitating an Online Meeting

According to research by Intercall, a conference and collaboration
service, conference call distractions include:

- 65% of people doing other work,
- 63% sending emails, 55% eating or making food,
- 47% going to the restroom, and
- lower percentages who text, check social media, play video
  games, or shop online instead of paying complete attention to the
  conference call.

"Hosting a Meeting is Easy... Holding Participants' Attention is Hard"
(Fraidenburg, Michael., 2020, p. 45). Facilitation is the solution.

> **Driving Principles:** 1. Engagement, 2. Relationships, 4. People
> Support What They Create, 6. Wasting Time

Good facilitation focuses on several things at once: primarily achieving the meeting's deliverables plus getting participants to contribute
to and buy into the decisions. You want people coming back for
more.

> *"They [facilitators] guide the participants towards an explora-
> tory journey of learning by helping them to delve into their in-
> ner self to realize their strengths and weaknesses, helping them
> to share their experiences and learning from the experiences of
> others."* (Akash Chander, 2014).

Keep eye contact by looking at the camera, not at the faces on the
screen when you are speaking.

> **Guideline 17:** The more facilitating, the less lecture, the better. Why? Because _**"People Support What They Create, not what you dictate."**_ You want attendees to _use_ what they get out of the meeting. They are more likely to do that if _they_ had a hand in creating the outcomes.

To facilitate means to help others. In this case, help them learn, help them achieve the deliverables of the meeting, and help them connect. While new information does need to be presented, learners need to assimilate it. The best way to do this is by keeping them engaged.

Face-to-face people would interact naturally and feel much more comfortable speaking up. People feel less comfortable speaking up because there's less trust in an online meeting until the people really know each other. There are fewer opportunities to talk because only one person can talk at a time. So, your job as the leader and facilitator is to help people regain that trust. Your job is to help them feel comfortable participating.

Here are some tips on how to do that:

✓ Get the participants to **engage in dialogue**.

- When you are asked questions, don't always answer them directly; instead, bounce them back to the other participants and keep the discussion going.
- Ask open-ended questions like, "Why would ...?", "How would ...?", "Under what circumstances would you ...?", "What do the rest of you think?" "What's next?"
- Direct questions to specific individuals instead of the whole group.
- Ask people to summarize what was just discussed or the decision reached.
- Ask questions to get more information, gain different perspectives, nail down areas of agreement and disagreement, clarify fuzzy areas.

✓ **Use a whiteboard or document** as your online flip chart to keep track of important points.

✓ **Ask** people or shake their head if they agree or disagree. Even this minimal action keeps them involved.

✓ **Keep the conversation on track.** "That is a great idea/question/issue/concern. Let's write that here in the Parking Lot for our next discussion."

  – But be careful. Sometimes that different line of thinking can be really productive. Evaluate if it has the potential of achieving the meeting deliverables by a different route or helping an unstated goal.

✓ **Keep people from monopolizing** the conversation by asking questions directly to people who have said little.

✓ **Actively listen** and then restate or summarize what people say. This lets them know you really did listen and confirms you heard them correctly.

✓ **Watch for people being distracted** and bring them back into the meeting.

✓ **Watch the time**. Judge whether more time is needed on the current topic. If it looks like a lot more time is required, ask everyone if they want to lengthen this meeting or schedule another one.

✓ **Pay attention to body language** and voice tone. Look for things that need more attention or at least to be acknowledged. In larger meetings, you may need help with this.

✓ **Don't be afraid of arguments**, but remember the first rule of interpersonal communication: "When friction occurs, ask each person to restate the other's point of view to the other's satisfaction before giving his or her side."

✓ **Bring closure to each item/topic** as it is covered. Summarize as needed. Make sure any decisions or plans are clear.

Task Meetings

It is more important in these meetings than in more casual meetings to stay on task and not wander off too far into personal stuff. People come to these meetings with the idea that they're there to get something done, not to socialize, so be sure to keep the meeting on track. You still need to keep people engaged and have time to build relationships, but that's not the meeting's focus.

Facilitator Tools

The Role of a Facilitator. https://www.mindtools.com/pages/article/RoleofAFacilitator.htm This site has a good set of tools for facilitators.

 Best Practice 13: Facilitate—keep people engaged and get as many people involved as possible while focusing on the deliverables.

Tips for Presenting Effectively Online

Guideline 18: **Present effectively to keep people engaged which will lead to better decisions and more learning.**

In some meetings like conference sessions or training courses, there will be a requirement for one person to present a fair amount of material in lecture form. But be aware. Lecture means people can only listen. (Just curious, do you like being lectured to? ☺) That would be fine if people would listen the whole time. But the human brain wants to wander, as we learned earlier in that thought experiment about relaxation. So, when the meeting does call for significant presenting/lecturing, what can you do in addition to all those things you considered when planning your agenda? Here are a few ideas:

- **Look directly at the camera**, not at the screen with the participants. Watch some professionals on TV. Where do they look? At the camera, which is perceived as looking directly at you. You keep someone's attention more when you look them in the eye rather than off to the side or somewhere else. *"Present to the camera lens: do not look at your screen. You might want to tape a colorful post-it note behind your camera to remind you where to look."* (Foley, 2020).

- **Try speaking from a standing position.** You project more power and energy when standing than just sitting. You move around a little. You tend to use more hand motions. To put it another way, you have more body language, and you communicate it better when you are standing.

Thought Experiment 5

Think for a moment about some powerful public speakers you have seen, live or better yet, on TV like Martin Luthor King. Were they sitting or standing? Could you see just the top half of their body or most of it? What did they do that made them so powerful? Make a few notes. See if these ideas would work for you.

- **Get excited!** Talk like you absolutely love what you are talking about.

- **Mix it up.** Use the props and presentation documents or videos you designed for your presentation.

- **Move back a little from the camera** so the audience can see more of you, including your hand gestures. The closer you are to the camera, the more people can see exactly where you are looking. So, when presenting, back up a little. Now, when you look at the faces on the screen, it will look more like you are looking directly at the audience (keeping eye contact) instead of looking elsewhere. You can even have your own podium if you want.

- **Try putting your speaker notes near the computer screen.** Have something like a music stand or a second screen off to your camera's left or right rather than have your notes lying on the desk. This keeps your eyes on the audience.

- **Long?** If your talk is long, have an overview at the beginning and a summary at the end. This will help people remember the key points and put them into action. And get their input in the middle.

- **Ask for feedback.** Face-to-face presenters can read and even hear the audience. They can see the full body language of the audience. Online it is much more difficult to determine people's reactions and then make adjustments based on how the audience perceives presenters. Images are much smaller, and you rarely see the entire body. You could be talking, and everyone is bored out of their mind, but you will have no idea. Ask people to nod their heads.

Raise their hand. Use the Clap Hand button or any of the other controls available.

- **Important: mute everyone when someone is presenting.** If you don't, then someone who's making some minor background noise like shuffling papers or talking to someone offscreen will become the focus of the meeting for a moment, distracting people from the presenter.

- **Clearly give control back to the host** or indicate you are finished. You can simply say something like, "Back to you, Jim." I once watched a presenter finish and then just sit there for about 30 seconds before the host realized he was supposed to take control back.

- OK, now for a tough one, **record yourself doing a short presentation**. What you're looking for is to make sure you're looking at the audience, and they can see your body language.

 Best Practice 14: Don't just sit in your chair and talk. Present like you are on stage, in front of a live audience. Follow the tips above.

Tips for Running Breakout Sessions

These take some attention to set up and start. Whoever does it may miss a little of the meeting unless you use all the automatic features. Here is one place where an assistant comes in handy. You may need to send messages to the rooms.

Some meeting apps allow breakout rooms to ask the host to join them to help clarify points. If you use this feature, be sure to let people know before they leave the main session.

Monitor Chat

As the host, you *must* be attending to chat messages during the meeting because people may be sending you messages like, "Can't hear you," "You are breaking up," etc. In small meetings, this is not a problem. In larger meetings, you probably should have someone monitoring the chat.

Be Careful Playing Music or Videos

 Warning 12: Background noise or unmuted participants can interfere with music or videos being shared.

At times you may want to mute all participants, such as when listening to music or watching a video. People may want to sing along, *but* their voices are most likely out of sync with the music due to delays on the internet. Other times, even if they are not singing, there could be background noise coming from one participant, like a dog barking.

If you are in a noisy environment, remember to mute your microphone too while it is playing.

When it is finished playing, close it first before ending sharing it with the meeting.

Have Tech Support

Below is a repeat of the list of the things tech support can do that I covered during design.

- Admit people in from the waiting room if you are using one.
- Text or call people who were invited but have not shown up.
- Mute all people or help them unmute themselves.
- Create breakout rooms, assign people to breakout rooms, and start the breakout room session.
- Send messages to the breakout rooms.
- Assist participants who may need help with audio or video or something else via Zoom chat, phone chat, or a phone call.
- Monitor chat and alert the meeting host to any issues such as people not being able to hear. Respond as needed.
- Possibly start/present/share music and videos.
- Monitor participants in gallery view, looking for people who have distracting things going on. Mute noisy people (crunching potato chips, a yelling child, a barking dog). If a fan is spinning or something is going on in the background, contact them and see if they

can make adjustments. Even if they can't for this meeting, maybe they will for the next one.

? Pause for a moment and do a quick self-check. How many of these ideas do you think would help you? It will give you an idea of how much difference they can make.

Step 3: Bring Complete Closure to the Meeting

Driving Principles: 3. What Gets Rewarded, 4. People Support What They Create

Bringing closure is very similar to what is typically done in face-to-face meetings. The main difference is that in online meetings, proper closure is more important.

Guideline 19: **Motivate by summarizing all that was accomplished and thanking people for their contributions**

Summarize what was accomplished, decisions made, or what was taught. This will ensure that people see their time was well spent. If you are summarizing a training session, make your summary be more like a job aid or checklist than like a list of topics covered.

Thank everyone for participating. Sounds unnecessary. Doing it will have people leaving the meeting at least knowing that they were appreciated.

Remind them **about** the **feedback** email you will be sending.

Common Problems and How to Solve Them

Common Problem 25: Video and audio are out of sync: The person's mouth does not line up with their words. The leading cause of lip-sync problems is that audio can be processed a lot faster than video, especially high-definition video. High-definition video requires more processing power. As a result, it takes longer to process than audio or standard-resolution video signals. Here are some things you can do:

- First, check your internet speed, as described above.
- Get as close as you can to your router.
- Turn Wi-Fi off on your device and then back on.
- Leave the meeting, close out the meeting app, and retry.
- Reboot your device.

Common Problem 26: No web camera: If your web camera isn't showing up, the first thing to do is check to ensure all other programs that use the webcam are closed. Zoom may not be able to use the camera if you've already given access to it in a different application.

Common Problem 27: Participants with distractions: Text or use chat to send the participant a message to reduce the distraction (turn off the fan, close the door, etc.).

Check out this link for more solutions to these problems and others.

https://www.digitaltrends.com/computing/common-problems-with-zoom-and-how-to-fix-them/

Critical Running-a-Meeting Success Factors

Just like with the planning treatment, there's a lot to do here, a lot to remember. Since you can't read this chapter while you're running a meeting, just have the checklist handy. Make notes about things you missed or weren't entirely clear about how to do. Then after the meeting, go back and read those sections. Repeat that process for the next meeting.

Here are critical success factors you need to attend to during your meeting to increase your success.

Factor	What You Need to Do
1. Facilitation	✓ Facilitate rather than lecture when possible to increase engagement and retention.
2. Preparation	✓ Be ready early. Practice anything new *before* the meeting.
3. Attention to Relationships	✓ Do all you can to help people connect and build trust.
4. Tech Support	✓ The larger the meeting, the more critical it is to have someone managing the technical details so you can lead the meeting.

Chapter 5

Treatment III: Follow Through to Keep Meetings "Suck-free"

The meeting is over, now what? I thought we were done.

 Warning 13: The essential follow-through items covered here are much more likely to get done after a face-to-face meeting than an online one. Make a concerted effort to make these happen.

Golfers don't stop their swing after they hit the ball. Pitchers don't stop their arm swing after they let go of the ball. Batters don't stop their swing after they hit the ball.

You aren't done either. Some things should be done after the meeting is over. Face-to-face you may do most of these without even thinking about them because you likely see these people after the meeting. People may drop by your office and pick up things or ask questions. You may bump into them at lunch and discuss how the meeting went. Not so online! They are physically disconnected from the meeting location and hence more so mentally.

> Driving Principles: 3. What Gets Rewarded, 4. People Support What They Create, 8. Follow-up

Checklist for Following Through a "Suckfree" Meeting

Step 1: Recap

☐ Make it clear what decisions/ideas/results were made, what was accomplished.

☐ Outline the next steps, including who is to do what by when.

☐ Recognize people for their contributions.

☐ Summarize what they should have learned or now be able to do.

☐ Distribute copies of any whiteboard or other document that was created.

Step 2: Get Feedback

☐ What worked for creating the deliverables?

☐ What didn't?

☐ What made this meeting a good experience?

☐ What could we change to make these meetings better?

Step 3: Give Feedback

☐ Give personal feedback to people who did well, contributed, etc.

☐ Give suggestions for next time.

The things you need to do are:

- Distribute outcomes of the meeting and follow up on the next steps.
- Get feedback on how the meeting went from their perspective so that you can make the next meeting better.
- Give feedback so people don't repeat their mistakes.

Step 1: Recap the Meeting

"The group already decided on the issue, right? Surely, everyone will remember, right? Think again. Too often, what's not written down gets lost." (Fraidenburg, Michael., 2020, p. 116).

Be sure that people remember and follow through. Distribute a summary of the meeting. Don't just send them the minutes. Here are some ideas for things to include in your recap of the meeting.

- Make it clear what decisions/ideas/results were made.
- Outline the next steps, including *who* is to do *what* by *when*.
- Emphasize what was accomplished.
- Recognize people for their contributions. Be as specific as possible. Don't just say "thanks everyone for ..." Instead, something more like, "John, clever idea about ..., Jane, thanks for taking on the ..., and that was a great report from ..."
- If the meeting's goal was for them to learn something, summarize what they should have learned or now be able to do. Do this in the form of a job aid, not a topic list.
- Distribute copies of any whiteboard or other document that was created or people contributed to during the meeting.
- Give a heads up about what kind of follow-up is planned or even just being considered.

Why do all this?

- The business reason is to get the decisions, plans, and follow-up actions by individuals in writing. This clarifies exactly what the decisions and plans were and who is to do what by when just in case someone had other ideas.
- By making it clear what was accomplished at the meeting, people feel a sense of success. This is a powerful but subtle kind of reward. They feel that the meeting made a difference. You didn't waste their time. They will feel like their time was meaningful.
- Since they were involved in achieving the deliverables, they are more motivated to implement the meeting's outcomes.

> **Guideline 20: Include accomplishments and recognize contributors in your recap of the meeting to ensure that the deliverables get implemented and the participants are motivated.**

Step 2: Get Feedback

Evaluate your success so you can do better next time. A couple of factors affect the quality and quantity of feedback you get.

Timing: The longer you wait, the less likely people will be to get it to you. Other stuff just comes up. Plus, the more time that goes by, the less they will remember.

Complexity: The simpler you make the feedback request, the more likely you are to get it (more feedback). But if you make it too simple, it will not tell you what you need to do to correct the problem. Here are the areas I recommended earlier:

Deliverables:

- What helped us create the deliverables for this meeting?
- What got in the way? What could we have done better?

Experience (how people felt about the meeting, how it was run):

- What made this a great experience?
- What could we change to make it better?

 Best Practice 15: Get your easy-to-complete feedback request out ASAP after the meeting so your next meeting will be even better.

Step 3: Give Feedback

Give *specific* feedback to any **presenters** you had. People want to hear they did a good job. And if you have any suggestions for improvement next time, remember, *"If you can't say something nice, say it nicely."*

If any participant needs some tips on the camera angle, lighting, their displayed name, distractions in their background, etc., be sure to let them know for the next meeting.

Did the Meeting Have the Intended Impact?

I feel I would be remiss if I did not at least mention this. It is no different than a face-to-face meeting, but it is so important I just cannot leave it out.

We tend to have too many meetings. The answers to the following questions will give you the *real* value of the meeting but getting them is non-trivial and a topic for another day. I am not talking here about how people liked the meeting or if the meeting deliverables were achieved. I am talking about answers to questions like these depending on the meeting's purpose. At least consider them and see if you can get some answers as time goes by.

For planning and decision meetings:
- Did those plans get implemented?
- How did those decisions work out? Did they have the desired result?
- Did people do the next steps? Did they have the desired effect?

For learning meetings (training, conferences):
- A week or a month later, do people remember the essential points they learned? If so, that is at least a start.
- The better question is, did their behavior change as a result of what they learned? *Do* they actually do things differently or do things they did not or could *not* do before? Do they make better decisions?
- And most importantly, did things get better because of their behavior change?

If you are getting negative answers to these questions, then maybe meetings are not the answer. What else could it be?

Critical Success Factors for Avoiding "Suckitis" During Follow-Through

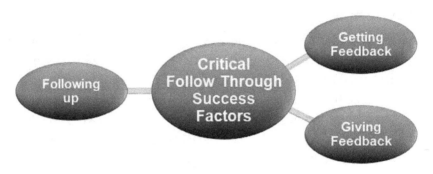

Factor	What You Need to Do
1. Following-up	✓ For all meetings, recognize people and identify successes. For important meetings, send out summaries of decisions, plans, and to-do lists.
2. Getting feedback	✓ Because we are on the bleeding edge of this technology with minimal experience to go on, the more quality feedback we can get, the better. ✓ Make it simple and easy to do. ✓ Do it ASAP.
3. Giving feedback	✓ Do it so others are motivated to help again and improve where needed.

Chapter 6

Key Remedies in the "Suckfree" Treatment Plan

There is a heap of stuff in this book. Here are the most important take-aways. These are the Driving Principles, Guidelines, and Best Practices in slightly different words.

If you remember nothing else from this book, remember this.

> **Do all you can to help people stay engaged, connect, build relationships, and trust each other.**

Don't try to put a round peg in a square hole. Online meetings may look like in-person meetings, but they are different. Treat them as such.

Key Remedies

Take Time to Plan Your Meeting

1. Plan your meetings.
2. Be clear about the meeting's purpose; have clear objectives and deliverables.
3. Keep meetings to a reasonable length. Include breaks in long ones.
4. Include ways to keep people engaged.

5. Design out distractions. Practice new features before the meeting.

6. Manage your risks.

7. Build in opportunities to connect and build relationships and trust.

Run Your Meetings Well

1. Go into your meeting prepared.

2. Get the technology wrinkles ironed out *before* the meeting, *not during.*

3. Facilitate, don't dictate. Get everyone involved.

4. Do all you can to help people connect and build relationships.

5. Stay on track.

6. Don't be too proud to have someone be your tech support.

7. Summarize accomplishments and thank people for participating.

Don't Quit After the Meeting

1. Follow-up after the meeting. Put accomplishments and "to-do's" in writing.

2. Learn from your mistakes—get feedback.

Back to the Beginning

Remember those questions I asked you to write down the answers to at the beginning of the book? The ones about what's wrong with your current meetings and what you'd like to do better. Well, take them out now and see how many of them have been covered by the book. If some did not get addressed well enough or at all, please send me an email, and I'll dig up the answers for you. BenPitman88@outlook.com.

Good luck with your next meeting. And remember, "the harder you work, the luckier you get."

Glossary

Technical Terms

App refers to any software application running on a device such as a phone, computer, or tablet. It includes things like Zoom, browsers, spreadsheets, word processors, etc.

Online meeting is a meeting conducted over the internet using video conferencing apps where people can see each other.

Virtual meeting is used as a synonym for online meeting.

People Terms

Conference all by itself refers to a meeting with a large number of people. Before Covid, these were usually association conferences with booths or meetings in large halls.

Conference call refers to a call with just a couple of people. Before online video, these were done on the phone. There is no agenda or prep. They were also called a teleconference. I tried to minimize the use of this term to avoid confusion.

Face-to-face and **in-person** are used as synonyms.

The **host** is the person running the meeting app. This is the term Zoom uses. I do not know what other apps use. The host has an account, sets the security, sends out the invitation, opens the meeting, etc.

The **Leader** is the person running the meeting. They may or may not be the host, the person who launched the app for the meeting.

Participant, attendee, and member are used interchangeably. While they do have slightly different meanings, they are used as synonyms in this book.

Presenter is the person presenting the current topic in the meeting.

Technical support person is usually a co-host for a larger meeting. The tech support person manages the technical side of more complicated meetings like breakout rooms and polls.

Webinar or **Web Conference** is an online meeting mostly focused on information sharing of some sort.

References

44-Icebreakers For Remote Teams. (2015, June 29). Retrieved from https://www.collaborationsuperpowers.com/44-icebreakers-for-virtual-teams/

Arthur, J. (2020). *Improve Your Virtual Meetings: How to Communicate from Anywhere, Master Video and Conference Calls, and Collaborate Like a Pro.* Kindle Edition.

Bacchus, A. (2020, November 10). *The most common Zoom problems and how to fix them.* Retrieved from https://www.digitaltrends.com/computing/common-problems-with-zoom-and-how-to-fix-them/

Bonnie, E. (2014, September 2). *7 Tips for Better Meetings* (Infographic). Retrieved from https://www.wrike.com/blog/7-tips-for-better-meetings-infographic/

Cerrato, A. (2020). *Online Meetings and Video Conferences: Look Like A Pro and Make The Most of Your Online Meetings.* Kindle Edition.

Chander, A. (2014, June 19). *6 Essential Skills of an Effective Facilitator.* Retrieved from https://www.linkedin.com/pulse/20140619061555-1334077-6-essential-skills-of-a-effective-facilitator

Chappell, L. & Spicer, G. (2020). *Virtual Event Survival Guide: Plan, Build, and Host Successful Online Events.* Laura Chappell University

DeBara, D. (2020, January 2). *The ultimate guide to remote meetings in 2020,* Retrieved from https://slack.com/blog/collaboration/ultimate-guide-remote-meetings

Facilitation Skills: Definition and Examples. (2020, February 4). Indeed Career Guide. Retrieved from https://www.indeed.com/career-advice/career-development/facilitation-skills

Ferrazzi, K. (2020, March 27). *How to Run a Great Virtual Meeting*. Retrieved from https://hbr.org/2015/03/how-to-run-a-great-virtual-meeting

Foley, K. (2020). *Virtual Meetings With Power And Presence: The Ultimate Guide To Online Meetings*. Kindle Edition.

Fraidenburg, M. (2020). *Mastering Online Meetings: 52 Tips to Engage Your Audience and Get the Best Out of Your Virtual Meetings*. CC Press. Kindle Edition. Excellent companion book. Has many tips for face-to-face meetings as well as online ones.

How to Run Effective Virtual Meetings. (n.d.). Retrieved from https://www.mindtools.com/pages/article/running-effective-virtual-meetings.htm

Kim, J. (2015, August 27). *8 Things That Always Go Wrong In Web Meetings*. (n.d.). Retrieved from https://www.insidehighered.com/blogs/technology-and-learning/8-things-always-go-wrong-web-meetings

Martins, A. (2020, June 3). *Tips on How to Avoid 'Zoom Burnout.'* Business News Daily Writer. Retrieved from https://www.businessnews-daily.com/15728-zoom-burnout.html

McCarthy, D. (2019). June 03). *9 Meeting Facilitation Skills for Managers*. Retrieved from https://www.thebalancecareers.com/meeting-facilitation-skills-2275915

Osman, H. (2020). *Better Online Meetings: How to Facilitate Virtual Team Meetings in Easy Steps* (A super-short book about what to do before, during, and after your remote meetings so that they're more effective). Kindle Edition.

Richards, P. (2020). *The Online Meeting Survival Guide: Learn Google Meet, Facebook Rooms, Microsoft Teams, Skype and Zoom*. Kindle Edition. This is one of the best books out there (besides this one) on online meetings. If you host many meetings, this is a book you need to read.

The 10 Most Common Video Conferencing Problems Explained. (n.d.). Retrieved from https://demodesk.com/blog/online-meetings/most-common-issues-explained

The Role of a Facilitator. (n.d.). Retrieved from https://www.mindtools.com/pages/article/RoleofAFacilitator.htm This site has a good set of tools for facilitators.

Wong, D. (n.d.). *How to Make Sure Your Next Web Conference Isn't a Complete Failure.* Retrieved from https://www.quill.com/content/index/computer-center/more-resources/make-sure-your-next-web-conference-is-not-a-complete-failure/default.cshtml. This is a good site with another way to look at conducting good meetings.

Zoom

There are plenty of free tutorials on YouTube.
- *Joining a Zoom Call for the First Time* (8:16) https://www.youtube.com/watch?v=9cxIZj8Wsk0&feature=youtu.be
- *Joining a Zoom Call on a Smartphone* (3:35) https://www.youtube.com/watch?v=_h7clS6eqv0&feature=youtu.be

Worth a Look

If you prefer books, here are a few I have reviewed:

Bernstein, J. (2020). *Zoom Made Easy: Establishing Lasting Connections (Computers Made Easy Book 17).* Kindle Edition.

Dale, M. (2020). *Zoom For Beginners: The Ultimate Guide To Get Started With Zoom And Other Conferencing Tools For Meetings, Business Video Conferences And Webinars Plus Tips And Tricks For Optimizing Your Video Calls.* Kindle Edition.

www.ingramcontent.com/pod-product-compliance
Lightning Source LLC
LaVergne TN
LVHW051246050326
832903LV00028B/2608